249.

Terry Philpot is editor of *Community Care* magazine.
He has edited several books, including *Social Work*
(1985), *Last Things: Social Work with the Dying and
Bereaved* (1989), *Practising Social Work* (with Chris
Hanvey) (1993), and *Values and Visions: Changing
Ideas in Services for People with Learning Difficulties*
(with Linda Ward) (in press) and has contributed to
others.

He is a member of the council of the NSPCC and was
formerly a member of the social work committee of
NCH Action For Children and of the advisory council
of the Centre for Policy on Ageing. In 1990 he visited
Czechoslovakia, as a British Council fellow, to look at
services for people with learning difficulties. He has
won a number of awards for journalism.

Action for Children

The Story of Britain's Foremost Children's Charity

Terry Philpot

A LION BOOK

This book is dedicated
to the staff of NCH Action For Children
and to all those with whom they work
and also to my mother,
who died as this book was nearing completion,
for my own childhood.

Copyright © 1994 Terry Philpot

The author asserts the moral right
to be identified as the author of this work

Published by
Lion Publishing plc
Sandy Lane West, Oxford, England
ISBN 0 7459 3136 7
Albatross Books Pty Ltd
PO Box 320, Sutherland, NSW 2232, Australia
ISBN 0 7324 1200 5

First edition 1994
10 9 8 7 6 5 4 3 2 1 0

A catalogue record for this book is available
from the British Library

Printed and bound in Great Britain
by Cox & Wyman Ltd, Reading

Contents

Introduction

At the beginning of 1994, as it prepared to celebrate its 125th anniversary, NCH changed its name. It became NCH Action For Children. Despite having moved up the hierarchy of voluntary child care societies to become the second largest after Barnardo's, an organization blessed with a name which had become almost synonymous with charitable work with children, NCH felt that its name did not mean much to the general public. While the term 'and Orphanage' had long disappeared from the organization's title, National Children's Home gave a wholly false impression of its work. (The change to the initials NCH was an unofficial name change which had been quietly inserted a few years ago to replace the National Children's Home.) There was much debate and consultation about the change (or development) of the name. A professional consultancy was called in, market research carried out, prompted and unprompted responses to what the existing name meant to members of the public analyzed, and the opinion of staff and supporters canvassed.

The organization's founder, Thomas Bowman Stephenson, had never, even in the earliest days, set out to found orphanages or institutions. He had probably seen too much of the Poor Law institutions to want to replicate such regimes. He intended (and succeeded in) setting up small, family-type homes, with half a dozen children in the care of a (significantly named) housemother and housefather. Ironically, the word 'home' used to describe such care came, over time, to mean the opposite—impersonal institutions.

But the changes in residential care for children since Stephenson's day were not the only reason why NCH wanted to change its name. The great majority of the work of NCH had not been residential for some while. Today, work with families takes place not only in its family centres but also mediation schemes for couples who are divorcing. NCH Action for Children is the largest single funder of mediation schemes in the UK (a service which continues to exist without any government funding). Fostering, adoption, family centres, work with homeless youngsters and those leaving care, alternatives to custody for young offenders, care for children who have been sexually abused—this constitutes the majority of its work in the 1980s and 1990s.

The plight of children were what had moved Stephenson and his associates, Alfred Mager and Francis Horner, and remained the organization's *raison d'être* 125 years later. While Stephenson is a far less well-known figure than his contemporary Thomas Barnardo and had none of the latter's flamboyance (but none of his shortcomings, either), as a pioneer in the care of children he deserves first place. It was perhaps no more than luck which allowed Stephenson to open his first home only a year before Barnardo. However, there are more important reasons why Stephenson's contribution to child welfare deserves greater recognition.

While Stephenson was motivated by his strong Christian faith, from which grew his hatred of injustice and suffering, from the very first he could see that good intentions were not enough. He abhorred any idea that the children should fall victim to the 'pious blundering' (as he called it) of those who cared for them. In the first homes he began elementary versions of what today would be recognized as residential child care training. As the Home grew so the training became more sophisticated and the Home founded a training school. Professor Roy Parker, in his history of child care[1], believes this to have been the one innovation in the work of the voluntary societies in the interwar years. When the Curtis Report on the care of children reported in 1946, training for residential care staff was unknown, apart from the training by the Home and Barnardo's.[2]

Consider also the history of the Home's involvement with child emigration (at first to Canada and later to Australia). This is now seen as mistaken, but none of the deliberate abuses associated with it have been laid by research at NCH's door.[3] Given the general standards of the day and the manner in which many children were treated, Stephenson and his successors appear enlightened. They attempted to ensure, in the difficult geographical and physical circumstances of those countries to which the children were sent, that continued supervision was a part of the Home's policy. Whatever the good intentions, however, of those who carried out this policy (and NCH's role, in terms of total numbers was a small one), the wholesale removal of children to often lonely existences in a country not their own, with people they did not know, must have been, in many cases, devastating and traumatic.

Today, residential care is unfashionable and frequently neglected but NCH Action For Children's work offers examples of what a positive factor it can be in the spectrum of care. At the same time, the organization's long and continuing belief in alternatives to residential care can be seen in the fact that, for example, it was one of the first to pay adoption allowances. That is but one historical indicator of the enormous range of community-based work which it undertakes today.

The organization's history of social concern continues to be matched by innovative practice. This book is, I hope, a testament to that. It is, in part, a history of the organization and being so, gives some idea of the great movement of ideas and practices and developments which has shaped child care generally these last 125 years. A portrait of such a remarkable British agency must, like those of its contemporaries—The Children's Society, Barnardo's, and smaller agencies—offer an illuminating commentary on the development not only in provision for children and young people, but also in how they have been viewed. A century or more ago, children were merely the chattels of their parents; now they are seen as individuals (whatever their age) with rights.

This long battle is far from won. The history of the treatment of juvenile offenders perhaps displays more than most how the pendulum swings back and forth—from the punitive to the compassionate; from a belief in the inherent badness of offenders to the idea that, whatever our personal responsibility as citizens, society and parenting shapes all of us. Today NCH Action For Children is the single largest provider of alternatives to custody projects. It is encouraging that when short-term supposed political advantage seems often to motivate those in power to talk about 'short, sharp shock' treatment or to favour locking up young offenders, bodies such as NCH Action For Children have continued to demonstrate that there are alternatives that work and, by so doing, keep the faith.

A large part of this book looks at the work of NCH Action For Children today by examining the policy context in which it works. It is also devoted to descriptions of twelve of its 215 projects. These show the scope of its work, both professionally, in the types of concerns it takes on, and geographically—from work with the Chinese community in Glasgow to supporting parents of children with learning difficulties in Wales. One cannot visit any of these projects without being impressed by the dedication of their staff, as well as the participatory role played by many of those who use the projects. It is right that this book should, in part, be dedicated both to those staff and those with whom they work.

There are a number of people whose advice and help I have valued. First, I would like to thank all the staff whom I have met and the users of projects who have shared their opinions and spoken of their difficulties and satisfactions. There are too many to name but many are quoted in this book, although anonymity for some users has been necessary. I wish especially to thank project leaders who offered helpful comments on their individual sections.

As to individuals, I wish to thank, in alphabetical order, Helen Dent, director of policy and information, who sought out some facts and figures for me. Dr Chris Hanvey, director of the Thomas Coram Foundation, gave helpful comments on the penultimate chapter and also took me through some contemporary statistics on child care. It was he, too, who, when assistant director of NCH Action For Children, first suggested that I might write this book. I would like to thank him for his early encouragement and for his ideas on the shape which the book might take. Bill Lynn, pastoral director, discussed with me how the organization has reconciled its Christian basis with its place in a multi-racial, multi-cultural society. Stan Newens MEP for Central London, who many years ago encouraged a schoolboy interest in history for which I am forever grateful, kindly cast an historian's eye over, and made suggestions, on chapters 1 and 3. I am grateful especially for the uncomplaining and very necessary help given to me by Chris Preddle, librarian at Highbury. I remember with especial fondness working in the quiet of the library on books and documents which he obtained either from his library's stock or from elsewhere. Chris Rowland, the archivist at Highbury, checked some facts for me. Dame Gillian Wagner, author of *Children of the Empire*, the indispensable work for anyone looking at child emigration, and of the classic biography *Barnardo*, was kind enough to read and comment on chapter 3. She offered much valuable criticism and caused me to consider this extraordinary social experiment from the point of view of the children. I hope that Dame Gillian will recognize something of her advice in the chapter. I have to offer especial thanks to Dr Linda Ward, senior research fellow, Norah Fry Research Centre, University of Bristol. She read a large part of the MS and her ever-perceptive comments on matters of style and construction saved me from many a solecism and stylistic infelicity. I owe her a considerable debt. Tom White, chief executive and principal of NCH Action For Children, read the manuscript and offered helpful comment and criticism. Ian Wratislaw, director of advocacy, gave me many insights into the increasing sophistication of attracting voluntary donations and corporate sponsorship.

While I extend gratitude to all the foregoing, matters of interpretation and responsibility for errors and omission rest with me.

Last, a word on nomenclature. I have used various terms to refer to NCH Action For Children. When it would generally have been known as the National Children's Home or the Home I have called it so. In more recent years, when it adopted the shortened form of NCH I have used that. I have made use of its new title to describe it and its work today.

Terry Philpot   Surrey, May 1994

1 | Methodism and its minister: religion for the poor

NCH Action For Children has its roots deep in the Methodist movement, whose founder, John Wesley, was, at first sight, an unlikely rebel. He had been brought up in the High Church rectory of his father in Lincolnshire, and had served as his curate. He was an Oxford don of 'high church views and unenlightened politics', as one historian has remarked, but despite this background he seemed to embody the spirit of seventeenth-century Puritanism—a personal piety—to many of his followers.[1] He did not see himself leading a breakaway denomination. And, like the term 'Quaker' for the members of the Society of Friends, 'Methodist' was originally a description which was used sardonically by its opponents.

Methodism was a movement marked by a life of religious devotion, self-discipline and work for others. It came partly as a reaction against the prevailing 'natural' religion of the early eighteenth century. The Age of Reason's religion was one of rationality: ideas of God could be comprehended without revelation, and it placed a growing emphasis on works rather than faith, a belief that Christians were those who lived a Christian life, and that charitable endeavour was its natural expression. But for the poor and the uneducated—those growing numbers who swelled the great industrial towns and cities—there was not much spiritual consolation in such beliefs. The Anglican Church toiled on in rural England, but floundered and fell behind in the newly created industrial cities. Its parish system was suited more to an agricultural society, and the Church's footing was unsteady in the fast-spreading industrialization and urbanization.

Wesley's mission

In 1738, at the age of thirty-five, Wesley, determined to devote himself to evangelistic work, found the churches closed to him. He and his followers took their religion to the fields and the street corners, in the great manufacturing areas and in the isolated mining communities. Preaching in the open air seemed to offer a threat to parish clergy. His mission to bring the idea of personal salvation to everyone, of whatever rank, and his belief in the democratic workings of grace, worried the squirearchy and the bishops. Yet his was not a politically radical movement—Wesley himself was a Tory and his methods of governing his body of lay preachers and followers authoritarian. But Methodism was a movement which challenged the Established Church, even though it remained a part of it until after Wesley's death in 1791.

Many charges were laid against Wesley and his followers. They were often mutually contradictory. Indeed, 'the sheer multiplicity of charges' laid against the Church 'makes it obvious that Wesley touched a tender spot on the contemporary conscience and exposed an embarrassing deficiency in its pattern of beliefs'.[2] Wesleyan Methodism did not challenge the social order, but what was to become a radical schism within Anglicanism reached to the unmet spiritual needs of an industrial working class. This was to be of profound religious, social and educational significance.

Early Methodism, in the words of another historian, was 'not a religion of the poor, but for the poor'.[3] Many of its parts were democratic, placing emphasis on organization—Wesley's great practical gift—which gave education, self-respect and administrative experience to working-class people. Schools in villages and market towns would be run by a Methodist committee when there were not Anglican schools. (Catholic schools, permitted since 1791, were much less common and there was no national system of education until 1870.)

Methodism itself was marked by frequent splintering. Before his death Wesley had left provision for a continuing 'Yearly Conference of the People called Methodists'. Within a few years of his death, Methodists were outside the Church of England. Six years later came the break from the Wesleyan Methodist Church of the Methodist New Connexion by Alexander Kilham, who had advocated a complete separation from the Established Church and was expelled by the Methodist Conference in 1796. The formation of the Independent Methodists was followed by that of the Primitive Methodists (1810), Bible Christians (1815), Wesleyan Methodist Association (1835) and the Wesleyan Reformers (1849). The later history, too, is often one of schism, and sometimes resulting allegiances and mergers. It was not until 1932 that Methodists were again united.[4]

There was, though, a common thread in many of the new Methodist manifestations. All were characterized by the evangelistic zeal of the movement's founder. Their mission was to the poorer classes, though, at the same time, they attracted the new middle classes, emerging from the great manufacturing and commercial concerns. Socially and spiritually, Methodism was a non-elitist, non-exclusive denomination.

John Wesley was politically conservative and there were those Methodist leaders and other prominent members who came after him who were to defend child labour and oppose the teaching of writing in Sunday Schools. But also (and particularly among Primitive Methodists) radical politics had a part to play. So, Methodism, as it grouped and regrouped throughout its history, was marked by variety.

Stephenson the Methodist

Thomas Bowman Stephenson, the founder of NCH, was quite literally born into Methodism. He was born in his father's manse at Red Barns, Newcastle-upon-Tyne, three days before Christmas in 1839.[5] He was the seventh child of his parents. His mother's health was poor, perhaps through much child-bearing, and he spent some of his early years in the care of an aunt. Thus, however close his extended family, he soon learned what it was to be separated from his immediate one.

His father, John Stephenson, had served as a preacher and minister in Lincolnshire, and, from 1823, had spent five years as a missionary in the West Indies. He had returned to England to marry Mary Bowman of Darlington, whom he had known before he had gone away and with whom he had continued to correspond. He had every intention of returning to the Caribbean after his marriage. But he was posted to a rather different island environment—the Shetlands.

Because of the way that Methodism organizes its ministry, young Thomas moved with his parents from church to church, circuit to circuit—Bedford, Lough, Dudley, Sheffield—as his father was directed. And so, the young Stephenson's eyes were opened to social distress—poverty, unemployment, hungry children, the problems caused by cheap, bad but consoling alcohol. Stephenson must also have recognized the gulf between the respectable, better-off people who made up the Sunday congregations to whom his father preached and life on the streets outside the church. The slums, the insanitary working conditions, the mean streets, the ugly chimneys of industrialism—he would have seen them or, perhaps, heard them discussed in the manse. Before he set off for his day at one of the series of grammar schools which he attended, his poorer contemporaries tramped to work in the early hours of the morning along dark, unpaved streets to factories, where they spent a long and gruelling day and where they might be seriously injured or even die.

In later years, Stephenson's relationship with his congregations was not always easy. This may be explained by his political radicalism—he was to speak for Liberal candidates when he served in his ministry in south London—and his methods of evangelization. And the explanations of these two aspects of his ministry can be seen in the kind of church and society to which he was heir.

Stephenson had been born five years after the passing of the Poor Law Amendment Act, which *The Times* had described in 1836 as 'that appalling machine ... for wronging the hearts of forlorn widowhood, for refusing the crust to famished age, for imprisoning the orphan in workhouse dungeons and driving to prostitution the friendless and unprotected girl'.[6] The Act had sought to abolish outdoor relief for the poor and the 'workhouse' test was imposed on applicants to divide the 'deserving' from the 'undeserving' poor. The idea was to make life in the workhouse less attractive than employment in field or factory. The standards of comfort in the workhouse were deliberately depressed to ensure that only those without other means of support were forced to enter it.

But there were contrary forces at work, too. *Oliver Twist* was published in the two years before Stephenson's birth. He was in his mid-teens when the other most marked of Dickens' novels of social criticism, *Bleak House* (1853) and *Hard Times* (1854), appeared. The great Reform Act had been passed in 1832, two years before the Poor Law Amendment Act, and had extended the franchise, albeit to a limited extent, and abolished the 'rotten boroughs'. In 1844 the Rochdale Pioneers' Co-Operative Society, the first of its kind, had come into being. Charles Kingsley, influenced by the Christian socialist movement, was writing, and Shaftesbury, an old-fashioned high Tory and evangelical, was active in social reform in Parliament. None of this could have passed by a young man whose father worked close to the conditions of his day, and who was himself becoming conscious of the world about him.

But Stephenson's first inclination was not to follow his father into the ministry. At school in Dudley he had—in a phrase he often used in his life—

'decided for Christ', and when he was at Wesley College at Sheffield he developed a taste and talent for public speaking. His first thought was not the pulpit, but the Bar. He went to London to study but, while on vacation at home on Tyneside (to which his parents had, by this time, moved back), he stood in for a minister who was ill. He intended the money he earned to pay his tuition fees. It was the congregations on Tyneside—some in the cities, others in villages—who, by their response to his preaching, brought his first calling onto question. His conviction grew and, in 1858, at the age of nineteen, he offered himself as a candidate for the ministry.

Stephenson had to travel to London to be interviewed by a committee of prominent ministers prior to any recommendation to the Methodist Conference that he be considered a candidate for the ministry. A month later he learned that he had been accepted. His next two years were spent at Richmond, one of the first Methodist theological colleges. When he left, he had nearly completed his BA and had experience of student preaching under the tutelage of some notable preachers. One of these was Dr Morley Punshon, who was to figure significantly when, later, Stephenson became involved in child emigration (see chapter 3). By now he had signed the teetotal pledge. Although it was the custom that port and ale would be offered to Methodist ministers who might have made long journeys, often on foot, across moors to preaching engagements, Stephenson remained a total abstainer all his days.

Taking faith to the people

In 1860 he took his first church in Norwich. It was a large and quite comfortable congregation. Despite his comparative youth and it being his first placement, he surprised his congregation by his unusual methods. For Stephenson, singing had been a love from his school days. By all accounts, he sang strongly and well. He had sung, unprompted, in the street when he had come to London for his interview for his candidature. Now he took to singing solo during the services which he conducted.

He also copied what he had seen in London: taking over a theatre for Sunday services to attract those who would go to the theatre but not think of entering a church. This innovation, though in keeping with the Methodist belief in taking faith to the people wherever they were, not only scandalized his congregation, but also raised eyebrows in the wider community. For many people, the theatre building was too redolent of its secular activities: the acts on the stage, the fighting, the catcalling, the kind of people who were thought to be attracted both to see the show and to act in it.[7]

In 1862 Stephenson found approval with his congregation. He took on in public debate Charles Bradlaugh, the most noted and publicly renowned non-believer of his day. Bradlaugh was the defender of Darwin, whose *The Origin of Species* had appeared only three years previously and had upset the accepted Biblical view of the origins of humankind.

That same year, reaching the end of his three-year ministry in Norwich, Stephenson went to a vastly different place, the Daniel Street chapel in Manchester. Here his political views would probably have been even less acceptable than in Norwich. Among his congregation were well-heeled cotton mill owners. Their new minister supported the Union forces in the American Civil War, then raging across the Atlantic. He spoke for the Northern States from his pulpit and when he did so at a public meeting at the Manchester Free Trade Hall, his removal was demanded. So far as the mill owners were concerned, the supply of cotton had dried up in the chaos that war had brought to the South. Their mills and their profits were of more concern to them than the abolition of slavery.

And, as in Norwich, Stephenson sought out those whom he did not find in the pews of his church. He opened the Daniel Street schoolroom on Saturday evenings—when some working people had free time and money to spend—for programmes of recitations and musical items, in which he himself participated.

In 1864 Stephenson was both ordained and married. His wife was Ellen Lupton, whom he had met eight years before. It was to be a long and happy marriage—she died twenty-two years before him in 1890. She appears to have played no great part in his public life, though she probably did all those things which a minister's wife was expected to do. She disliked London and would have preferred a life in a northern industrial manse. But, in the custom of the times, when she was not assisting him, in ways which have not been recorded in much detail, her life was given over to bringing up their daughter, Dora, and homemaking.

Later, when the Home was founded, it took boys only, and Ellen Stephenson took a small girl into their home until the House for Girls was available. She then spent time caring for the children at the Home, at one time conducting a weekly religious meeting for the girls. Bradfield, Stephenson's biographer, says that 'she was of a very quiet and retiring disposition, and the publicity and restlessness of his career was at first a great difficulty to her. She would have been entirely happy as the wife of a quiet circuit minister, who trod the path of duty faithfully from one ordinary appointment to another'.[8]

Despite the protests caused by Stephenson's political activities, he stayed in Manchester and the Stephensons' third year there was spent in Droylesden when the circuit was reorganized. Their next move was to Bolton. This was, perhaps, a congregation more to Stephenson's taste: it was working class with an active church community, and a large Sunday school which, in the fashion of Lancashire[9], took in all ages.

But here, too, he took the church to those who did not come to it—for three winters he organized (at 2d entrance fee) 'open evenings'. Those attending had a cup of tea and a bun. There was music and lectures by politicians, writers and scientists; it was attractive enough to warrant an average attendance of 500 over these years. He also organized a mission in an area where there was no physical presence of the church with regular open-air meetings[10] and a magazine called *Monthly Greetings*.

Bolton, under Stephenson's encouragement, was also one of the first five circuits to have youngsters collect money for a new scheme that was to become the Juvenile Missionary Association of the Methodist Missionary Society. He employed a 'a woman worker', and even called her a deaconess, prefiguring the Order of Sisters which he was to found as part of the work of the Home. His social concerns (though Stephenson would have made no distinction between his faith and his social responsibilities) were expressed in a savings bank, associated with the church, for working people, and literacy classes.

In 1868 it seemed that the Stephensons would spend their next three years in Leeds, having been invited by the congregation, in the manner of Methodist practice. But he was sent to Lambeth to take charge of the Waterloo Road chapel, which stood where the Union Jack Club can now be found. Nearby was the New Cut, a place notorious for crime and poverty. Stephenson cast his eye about: he saw the slums, he looked at the street markets, he saw the people hurrying across nearby Waterloo Bridge and he knew he had little hope of local people being induced to come to his chapel. And so, on the ground outside the chapel, which stood some way back from the road, he erected a platform for open-air meetings. Believing that his new and hoped-for congregation was more likely to listen and to stay if they could sit down, he launched an appeal among Methodists for £50 to buy 200 chairs. The meetings were held each evening and on Saturdays there were 'newspaper evenings' when news items were read to an audience many of whom would not have been able to read or write.

But there was something else which tugged at Stephenson's well-developed conscience. He had always been concerned about children, and especially pleased when many teenagers had turned up for the winter evening events in Bolton. He had said that had he stayed in the north he would have done something for children [11], although he does not appear to have had any firm idea of what that something might have been. In Lambeth the needs of children were obvious every time he left the manse. They were overworked, poor, abused, abandoned, orphaned, and in ill health. They were commodities, who did not know what childhood was.

There was no public service for children except for the oppressive workhouse. Compulsory education was still two years away and free universal schooling twenty years off. Stephenson was later to write of this time:

Here were my poor little brothers and sisters sold to Hunger and the Devil. How could I be free of their blood if I did not try to save some of them? I began to feel that my time had come. [12]

2 | In the beginning: the first home

By 1869, Thomas Bowman Stephenson was sufficiently well known and respected that two Methodist Sunday School secretaries, Alfred Mager and Francis Horner, wishing to raise money for a model lodging house for homeless youngsters in Southwark, asked him to lend his name to the project.

The Farmhouse

Mager and Horner, friends and colleagues at the Clifton Street Sunday School, had seen the poverty and destitution of the young in the notorious 'Mint' area and had come upon a property called 'The Farmhouse' which they wished to buy and convert to a lodging house. The two men already had another connection with Stephenson, apart from the local circuit: Mrs Mager knew Ellen Stephenson. At thirty-two, Mager was two years older than Stephenson and eight years Horner's senior. Horner, who was Irish, was beginning a career in business, while Mager, who had risen rapidly in banking, assisted by a legal training, was the son of a Bath councillor and Poor Law guardian.

Horner's experience was similar to the celebrated story about Thomas Barnardo, who, dining with Lord Shaftesbury, and being challenged to find street boys, went with him and two others and found seventy-three of them sleeping rough in Lower Thames Street.[1] Horner had gone, just before midnight, to London Bridge (no distance from Lower Thames Street) when snow was on the ground and had asked a policemen if he knew of boys sleeping rough. He was taken to a landing pier where a large tarpaulin was raised to reveal boys, shoeless, ragged and miserable; among them were two brothers whose mother was dead and whose father had deserted them.

But Stephenson wanted to play a more active part than lending his name to an appeal in the *Methodist Recorder*. As he was later to state: 'A few months after my coming to London, circumstances occurred which appeared to me an indication of God's will in the matter.' Stephenson met with Mager first and suggested a somewhat different venture. Mager wrote to Horner:

Dear Horner
Come tomorrow to tea with us. Mr. Stephenson has called to talk
with you and me upon a new and interesting subject.
Yours affectionately, Alfred W. Mager.

This 'new and interesting subject' was the proposal by Stephenson that the three of them should found, not a model lodging house, but a home for boys who did not have one, where training could be offered in the principles of Christianity, together with industriousness.

In this social concern the three men were in step with their times. A great evangelical revival had taken root in Northern Ireland at the time when Stephenson had been housed in his first manse. The effects of the revival, though less in terms of conversion, had been felt elsewhere in the kingdom. The evangelicals knew that hunger and despair were fierce competitors with the life of the spirit. And so, by a desire to remove the material and physical barriers to spiritual well-being, extensive charitable work was undertaken.

The efforts of Thomas Barnardo, begun a year after the founding of the home by Stephenson, Horner and Mager, are a well-known example of this work—to take children from the streets and put them in homes was to give opportunity for religious instruction and the acceptance of the gospel, and, thus, the conversion of all people. This was the particular mark of evangelicalism. It was for this reason, according to Barnardo's biographer[2], that his fund-raising was so successful.

Stephenson, as a Methodist minister, had the spiritual welfare of everyone—street boys, as much as the more respectable members of his congregation—at heart. But while he spoke at times in strongly missionary terms, his belief in the need to reach the souls of the youngsters taken into his care was much less pronounced. However, there is no way of knowing what was to motivate those who gave money to the Home. Their motives were no doubt mixed, but money was money and it was used to put a roof over heads that had been covered by tarpaulin, and food in stomachs that had been empty.

But as well as the continuing influence of the religious revival, there were other forces at work. By the end of the century, these were to bring about great change through legislation and charitable endeavour. Homelessness among the young was not the only cause for political concern, even if it was the most visible. Until the second half of the century, children who were placed with private foster-parents had no legal protection, nor were they subject to any more supervision from the law or statutory agencies than children who remained in their own homes. There was a series of scandals involving parents farming out children, giving away or even selling their children, and neglect in the homes to which they went. This led, in 1870, to the founding of the Infant Life Protection Society, and two years later to the passing of the Infant Life Protection Act, under which, private foster-parents (usually mothers) who took in more than two children for some kind of payment, whether in cash or kind, would be required to register with the local authority.[3]

And three years before Mager and Horner met with Stephenson, the Children's Employment Commission had shown how the legislation to protect chimney sweeps had proven ineffectual, rendered null through the connivance and failure of magistrates, private householders and local authorities to make it work. It is this campaign which is forever associated with the name of the Earl of Shaftesbury. He, perhaps more than anyone, personified the spirit of the socially concerned, wealthy evangelical.[4] Six years after the meeting of Mager, Horner and Stephenson that particular evil was ended when Shaftesbury introduced a Bill into the Lords, following the death of fourteen-year-old George Brewster, when sweeping a flue at the Fulbourn Lunatic Asylum, near Cambridge.

In 1866, under the auspices of the Ragged School Union, Shaftesbury had given his support to the idea of setting up training ships to help the homeless boys of London. This had long been a concern of his: in 1848 he had attempted to secure £1,500 from Parliament to assist juvenile emigration (see chapter 3). His Bill in the Lords in 1853 had allowed children found begging to be brought before the magistrates for committal to the workhouse. In 1868, the year in which Stephenson went to Southwark, William Charles Spurgeon had drawn crowds at his meetings at a new church, the Metropolitan Tabernacle in Newington Causeway, and had been given £20,000 by a wealthy female follower to found an orphanage.

The Children's Home

In such a ferment of social concern and deep religious feeling, Horner, Mager and Stephenson set to work. Within three months of their meeting, George Oliver—who until the day he died signed himself as 'G Oliver No 1'—and

Frederick James Hall were the first inhabitants of The Children's Home at 8, Church Street, around the corner from Stephenson's Waterloo chapel. Its official title was appropriately matter-of-fact for the premises which had been taken. 'The Farmhouse' was merely a former stable, with a loft and one downstairs room. A contemporary photograph shows it before conversion: a dog sits below a ladder leading to the loft, while a horse harness hangs from a wall, and a farm cart takes up much of the lower quarters. An early historian of the Home, the Rev. Nehemiah Curnoch, who had been a candidate for the ministry with Stephenson, when both had attended interviews at Westminster, wrote:

> *A more prosaic place could scarcely be imagined. The street—its name has been changed to Exton Street—is close to the railway arches which cluster around Waterloo Station. It is by no means the brightest street in a not very brilliant neighbourhood. An entry (now figuring as a wide doorway) was the only playground. A stable behind served as a dining room. Wood chopping was the only industry. A loft to the rear became a dormitory for the boys. A white mark on the wall of the higher building shows the spot at which the wash house was erected.*[5]

The boys were received into the Home (with the help of a Mr Callister, Stephenson's co-superintendent at the Waterloo Road Sunday School) on 9 July 1869. The three pioneers lost no time in promoting their new project. Ten days later the premises were used to host (and George Oliver and Frederick Hall to promote) an appeal for wealthy, potential supporters. A record of it, given in a pamphlet for well-wishers, stated that the object of the Home was 'to rescue children who, through the death or vice or extreme poverty of their parents, are in danger of falling into criminal ways'.

By the time the meeting took place, a six-person 'Council of Advice and Aid' and a four-person committee, which included Mager and Horner (Stephenson was listed as 'honorary director') had been formed. A Mr and Mrs Austin were given as being 'in charge of the Home' and listed as 'father' and 'mother'. Their titles evidenced the founders' intention to make the place homely and domestic. 'We do not desire to establish an institution', stated Stephenson.[6] The Austins received a joint weekly salary of £1 6s 6d (£1.32).

An appendix to the pamphlet, intended as instructions for the 'father' and 'mother', stated that they were to 'surround them [the boys] with all the influences of a Christian home', to realize, and make the boys realize, that they were one family. They should think of themselves always as heads of a family, and encourage the boys to treat them with the respect, confidence and affection due to parents. A mixture of 'firmness and wisdom and love' alone justified the assumption of the parental titles. No serious punishment was to be inflicted without consulting the director; family prayers were to be said morning and evening; the houseparents themselves would purchase articles and food needed for the home, and make and mend the boys' clothing. There would be no segregation (although how this could be otherwise in so small a premises it is difficult to see) so that they would all take their meals together. 'At their meals,' said the instructions, 'let them be merry and cheerful, but repress rudeness and boisterous conduct.'

Each boy should make his own bed and clean his own boots, and should help with housework, cooking and waiting at table. Strict attention was to be paid to the hours of school work, teaching, rising and 'industrial occupations'. Sunday would be kept as a day of rest and it was expected that chapel would be attended twice. During the day the boys could be given 'illustrated books', hymns could be sung, stories told, a Bible lesson given in the afternoon. 'Try to make the day the most attractive of the seven, while taking care that it is reverently observed.'[7] The houseparents were instructed to watch their tempers, their words and their deportment, and 'above all things, give heed to personal piety.'

Stephenson had been influenced in the regime at Waterloo Road by 'the home principle' of Dr Wichern at the *Rauhe Haus*, near Hamburg. Wichern had gathered children in 'families', living in separate houses, with a common school and common workshop, as opposed to offering large, impersonal institutional care. For people like Stephenson there was a reaction against the impersonality of the workhouse and 'the home principle' was to be a pervasive one in voluntary child provision. Barnardo, for example, was to create what amounted to a small village at Barkingside, Essex.

Stephenson pointed to the advantages:

> *It checks, if it does not entirely prevent, the evils so frequently found in very large gatherings of children—evils against which special precautions are needed, when the previous habits and associations of the children have been so foul. It renders maintenance of discipline possible without crushing the spontaneity and vivacity of child-life. It secures an exactness of oversight and a dealing with individual temperaments according to their special peculiarities,*

which, in other circumstances would not be possible; and it reproduces, as nearly as may be, that home-life which is God's grand device for the education, in the best meaning of the word, of the human race. There are, moreover, economic advantages attaching to this system, very important but of which I need only mention one. It enables the institution to be established without any enormous outlay for buildings, allows it to grow naturally, and by a succession of comparatively easy efforts, house being added to house, as the families multiply. Of course in our experiment, we could only begin on a small scale—in fact, with one family; but the essential principles of the scheme are being carried out there.

The fund-raising pamphlet went on to elaborate the objectives of the Home, which were:

to shelter, feed, clothe, educate, train to industrial habits, and, by God's blessing, lead to Christ, children who are in danger of falling into criminal habits. It is commenced in humble dependence on the blessings of Almighty God, and it is hoped that its daily engagements will be pervaded by a religious spirit. For it is the firm faith of its founders that good citizens can only be found in good Christians, and that Christian philanthropy should aim at nothing less than the conversion of the soul from sin to God.

This Institution is not for orphans only; in some cases children with both parents living are in a worse condition than if they had none. It prescribes no limit of age or circumstance in the applicants, but the Committee will judge of every case presented to them on its merits.

After stating that 'the cumbrous mode of election' to vacancies in the home would not be adopted but that members would pay 'the utmost deference' to the recommendations of any subscriber, and reckoning that in London about 100,000 children ought to be in the care of such an institution, it went on: 'As far as possible the feeling of independence will be cultivated among the boys.' The boys (there was no intention, as yet, to take in girls) were to receive wages for their work, which would be saved in the Penny Bank. Out of this they would pay a proportion for their clothing. Thrift and industry were to be encouraged.

This first appeal stressed that the Home was not a sectarian venture but one to be commended to the Methodist community. John Chubb, a member of the

Council of Advice and Aid, chairing a public meeting on the Home's behalf in February 1870, said that it 'had a special claim upon Christian people who had gone out to the suburbs to live, and who, now that their labours and influence were withdrawn from the centre of the town, ought all the more liberally to contribute their money to aid in the evangelisation of the masses of our fellow countrymen'.

The rental on the property was £40 a year and the running costs were put at £250–300 a year with repairs and fitting the property out with an additional £25 and furnishing for the first six boys at £15. Furniture, books and clothing were requested. There was even an early example of the financial sponsorship of children sought by some modern (mainly overseas) charities—one boy's accommodation could be paid for with £1 5s (£1.25). Six of the Home's first supporters gave £20 each.

Admissions

Just as the Home was not slow to promote itself, it was also rigorous in its record-keeping. The houseparents were to keep a ledger of all incidents. On reception, all boys saw a doctor for medical examination, and if suffering from skin or other diseases, were sent to hospital before being allowed to mix with other members of 'the family'. From the very beginning particulars of the children were taken meticulously on blue application sheets. Here were registered details of health; parental earnings; information as to baptism and legitimacy; and whether the child or parents had been to prison, in a workhouse, or had attended day or Sunday school. A final section dealt with 'habits', which were often recorded cryptically, and there were often highly subjective character assessments of both child and parent. Information was then recorded in a ledger, and then again in an admission book, to which, over the years, other information was sometimes added. Here, too, were sometimes pasted 'before and after' photographs of the youngsters. The first would frequently show a ragged, unhealthy-looking waif; the other a clean, well-dressed, occasionally self-conscious young person.

The mother of George Oliver, the Home's first inhabitant, like other parents (when they could be found), signed a form upon his admission. It is a simple scrap of paper, looking almost as if it were torn from a child's exercise book. It bears no heading and has no indication of legal status. It states simply: 'I hereby commit George Oliver to the care of the Director and Committee of the Home [indecipherable word] and Industry. I promise not to interfere with the management of the child's education; and I promise to remove the child whenever requested to do so by the Committee.' Mrs Oliver's 'X' is appended and witnessed.

In the ledger her son's date of birth is given as 10 March 1859 and continues: 'F. dead. Was porter at Beer Stores. M does Needlework. 6/- [30p] weekly. Boy, truthful, hot-tempered and swears.' Later additions indicate George Oliver's journey through the Home's care: 'Went to Edg [Edgworth, which opened in 1872] with the first group.' The admission book shows that George had a brother and two sisters. He had been to a Ragged School for a few months. 'Fairly truthful,' it remarks, adding: 'Healthy and of good intellectual capacity.' In 1872 he was apprenticed to a carpenter. His affection for the Home continued, shown not only in his pride in being 'No 1' but also in the correspondence with the Home which he kept up over the years, though this was often to regret that illness would prevent him from attending annual reunions and founder's day meetings.[8]

Girls were not excluded for long; indeed, the difficulty of accommodating them had been recognized from the start. But within a month of the opening of the Home the director and his wife had taken a girl into their own home until accommodation could be found for her.

The Home was soon attracting the attention of outsiders. A writer in the *New Zealand Methodist* gave a somewhat colourful account, complete with the alleged dialogue of chirpy Cockney street boys ('My, ain't it jolly'; 'Oh, sir, it was werry good, it was'. 'It was all about a cove wot had two kids, and one of 'em was a bad un' says one boy, asked about the last book his mother had read to him). The writer, who visited at Christmas, six months after the Home had opened, found it 'always clean and tidy', and gaily hung with seasonal decorations and complete with Christmas tree. Despite the sentimentality and mawkishness of the descriptions, the boys' happiness and the relaxed atmosphere is evident.[9]

In the ledgers, 'creed' is very often given as 'undeclared' and where it is noted it tends to be as 'Wesleyan' or 'Wesleyan Methodist'. The Home came officially under the wing of the Methodist Church in 1871 but that made no difference to the non-sectarian admissions policies which had been adopted from the beginning. But what was it that brought the youngsters to the attention of Stephenson and his colleagues? Poverty is the common thread that links all their stories. For example, Richard was fourteen and had parents who were 'great drunkards'. He himself had been in prison for three years for unspecified crimes, and was 'going to the bad fast'. He came to the Home after running away to sea.

When deserted by their mothers children were often unable to cope on their own. Some children, like the boy who slept under the arches for weeks before being found, were deserted by both parents. Sometimes a relative had taken them into their care and then had been too elderly or poor to look after them. The records are replete with references to illness and disability. A father was 'disabled for life'; there was 'ill health', 'declining health'; a parent was 'a cripple'; 'F insane' or 'in Lunatic Asylum', another 'a great invalid'. Industrial injuries were recorded, as was death. There was the case of the soldier judged 'not right' after returning from the campaign in the Sudan. 'M far gone in consumption', says an entry, as well as 'F a labourer but partially paralysed.'

The parents' supposed moral shortcomings were often referred to. One woman was 'suffering from venereal disease through father's misconduct'. 'Illeg' as well as 'M a prostitute' are frequent entries. One father had spent eight years in prison for forgery, another had died in Portland Prison; his wife was a 'depraved, vicious creature' with 'ragged and filthy children'. One father had been hanged for murder, another found guilty of the same crime. There were children living in conditions of 'great moral peril'. There was the mother who was 'a noted bad character'. One girl was sleeping with her father [10], while a mother was called 'a drunken woman of the worst type'. 'F (market porter) drunken, miserable jailbird' says an entry, and one mother was an evangelist who 'fell through drink'.

But many of the parents' virtues were also recorded. Here one suspects that the helper saw them struggling against great odds that were seen to be outside of their control and not attributable to any personal failings or inadequacies. There was 'M [who] was seduced and on the point of going on the streets when rescued by a midnight [religious] meeting'. Other entries seem to indicate that the parent has found his or her way back from the wayside, as when it was noted: 'M now a Bible-woman.' There were cases where both parents were seen to be 'steady and industrious'. After a birth an unmarried mother 'did her best to redeem her character'. Another woman who had a child while unmarried died two years later and the ledger says of her: 'Before her death professed conversion through the instrumentality of a Wes [Wesleyan] minister.' There was a 'good Christian, sadly overworked' and the woman who 'after seduction led a respectable life'. A prostitute seemed to have redeemed herself by marrying 'a respectable mechanic'.

Positive attributes of children are rarely recorded (though the records are more concerned with the ways of life, characters and attributes of the parents). A child is said to be 'bright and active' but this is qualified with the statement: 'but dirty and neglected'. But that is a rare entry. Children are not always seen as the passive victims of their parents' or social neglect. One boy, of unstated age, had spent two years at an industrial school before coming to the Home.

The testimonial from the school's governors noted only that he was 'incorrigible, a thief, a liar, a gambler etc'. Children being 'untruthful, dishonest and depraved' are common entries, as are those which record children as being 'beyond control'.

There was not much recording of unemployment but parents are frequently said to be dead, ill or deserting. Mothers often worked but for no great reward. Livings, such as there were, were said to be 'precarious'. There was 'great poverty ... recorded' in homes where there was work, just as often as where there was none. 'Begging' is not an uncommon entry, prostitution among children less so (though one twelve-year-old girl had three sisters, all of whom were prostitutes). So far as wages are concerned, in 1873 a braider was being paid 9s (45p) a week, a needlewoman 2s (10p), a washerwoman and a char 5s (25p), a tailoress twice that sum. A few years later a labourer, a cabman and an embosser were each being paid 18s (90p) a week, a shoeblack 2s 6d (13p) a week. An army pensioner got 4s (20p), while an industrial injury brought in 10s (50p). A carriage lamplighter could earn 12s (60p).

Sometimes children worked (though the ledgers did not record their incomes) by selling matches or doing similarly menial jobs. Parents were often dependent upon their children financially. One child was thrown out of a friend's house where he had gone after his mother's death, because he could not earn his keep. Where a child brought in no money, destitution was sometimes the result. But few cases were as extreme as the father who presented his son at the Home on the express understanding that he would be 'emigrated immediately' (he went to Canada). A mother came to the Home with three children wanting to save them from their father's (unspecified) bad example.

Cases of physical abuse are given but rarely described. There was a girl of drunken parents who was admitted with a black eye, several bruises and burns. 'Seemed to be idiotic and untruthful and dishonest. Found to be subject to fits', the entry laconically and unfeelingly reports. She was found a new home. One father had kept his children locked up and they ate only because neighbours passed in food on a clothes prop. One entry states: 'M and brutal stepfather utterly neglect boy. Afraid to go home at nights. For 7 weeks slept in fish tub under the Elephant and Castle.'

The story of eleven-year-old Alice Barbard and her sisters has almost a Dickensian pathos in its portrayal of family tragedy. 'F a sailor who returned from his last voyage in time to see his wife die, leaving three little girls. In the evening of the funeral F visited M's grave and returned home shattered in body and mind. A long and painful illness followed a short convalescence. Then he died and was buried at sea.'

There were exceptions to the poor who turned up on Stephenson's doorstep. There was the eighteen-month-old baby boy, 'the child of a young lady who was most cruelly and shamefully abused. The child was removed from the mother directly after birth and she has never known him. Her family very anxious that the matter should be kept a secret, and Dr S [Stephenson], knowing all the circumstances, consented to receive him on the understanding that he should be at liberty to dispose of him as he thought best.' When the boy was four he went to Canada.

Such cases meant that the Home expanded rapidly and at the annual meeting of January 1871 (less than two years after the first two boys had been received into Church Street), the neighbouring house had been taken and twenty-nine boys were now in the Home, most of them orphans. 'Some of the boys,' Stephenson told his audience at the meeting, 'give evidence of a truly rebellious feeling.'

As the records show, the children who came into the Home's care in the early days did so by being brought by their parents or referred by individual well-wishers concerned for a child, or were come across by Stephenson and his helpers. However, before long this practice and what has continued to be the notion of rescuing children off the streets was 'replaced in reality by complicated networks of referrals that make it difficult to know exactly how children came to be in the care of the voluntary agencies, upon whose initiative, and with what financial implications'.[11]

These networks were various. While the agencies looked unfavourably on the Poor Law, it was the Poor Law which was sending them increasingly large numbers of children. The Catholic rescue agencies actually began actively to invite the Poor Law guardians to send Catholic children in their care to them, being concerned in particular about the 'leakage of faith'—that Catholic children, subjected to Protestant and secular influences, would be lost to the Church. Stephenson appears to have received relatively few children by this route, unlike his counterpart William Rudolf at the Waifs and Strays (The Children's Society), who admitted a steadily increasing proportion.

The motivation of the Poor Law guardians was mixed: it was sometimes cheaper to transfer children to voluntary societies, rather than to build new homes; some societies (including Stephenson's) had developed specialist services for children who were disabled or sick and it was not economical for the Poor Law to provide these. Another reason was the desire of the guardians to ensure that that those for whom they were responsible in the longer term did not become dependent on their provision, seeking it out when they came upon hard times in adulthood. There was also the fact that some guardians wished the children to be sent abroad but had no organizational method of doing this (see chapter 3).

But the Poor Law was not alone in making use of the voluntary agencies in this way. With the expansion of its work in the 1890s, the National Society for the Prevention of Cruelty to Children, with no long-term care of its own, turned to them. The Probation Service was set up in 1907 and some probation officers saw older children were more likely to be supervised effectively in homes run by these agencies. As is to be expected, these traits continued through the first decades of the lives of the child care voluntary agencies.[12] In 1946, the Curtis Committee recorded that 4,500 Poor Law children were cared for in voluntary homes, or 16 per cent of the total population of such institutions.[13]

But whatever the reasons Stephenson's idea caught on so quickly, the early successful fund-raising did not continue to accompany it: a few months before the annual meeting in January 1871 the public's attention (and its donations) were attracted by the Franco-Prussian War and the Prussian occupation of Paris. Stephenson himself travelled to the battlefields and got as far as Vienna (see chapter 4). He returned from his European foray mindful of the fact that even with the expansion that had taken place, the premises were inadequate and at the 1871 annual meeting he had linked this to the want of a 'girls' department'.

Bonner Road and Edgworth

When Stephenson came back it was also to an invitation to join the Bethnal Green circuit, to move from the south to the east of London, to an area whose problems would be all too familiar to him. It was here now that he looked for new premises and he found them quickly, if unexpectedly, in Bonner Road. The rent was £190 a year. It was a small factory for the manufacture of paving stones in what had been a row of three-storey houses. The work of converting the premises fell to the officers and the boys—painting, glazing, laying floors, making drains, putting up party walls. Bringing in contractors to do the work was impossible for Stephenson did not know 'whether the Lord would send the money with which to pay'.

On 4 October 1871 the formal opening of Bonner Road took place, attended by, among others, Thomas Barnardo, whose own work was already beginning to be known. The premises could take 100 youngsters; by the time it opened there were already thirty-seven boys and six girls to live there.

The Children's Advocate said of the new Home:

> the ground (about half an acre in extent) may be described as an
> irregular pentagon, surrounded on four sides by buildings, and these
> buildings are the more interesting from the fact that they nestle
> under the protecting wing of the Methodist chapel. They consist of
> four 'blocks', with windows overlooking a fine piece of ground... As
> you enter the gates, on the right hand side is the first block, and here
> at once you come to the children's classroom... Above this is their
> 'chapel'... Further on, in the same block is the kitchen, furnished
> with the children's kitchener [sic] from Church Street, and likewise
> some boilers...Above the kitchen are the 'Father' and 'Mother's'
> rooms, many of the children's bedrooms, and a lavatory, playroom
> and general dining-room. The second block is to be devoted to the
> reception of girls. Beneath the upper portion is the covered
> playground for the children, where they may engage in athletic
> exercises... Here, also, are a bathroom and laundry. The third
> block... is apportioned in its lower compartment, to a carpenter's
> shop, where the lads are taught a useful trade; in its upper to the
> bedrooms of many of the children, with lavatory, & c., as in the first
> block which is called the 'Old Home'. The fourth block, to the left of
> the entrance gates, contains offices, bedrooms above for girls, and a
> few little beds marked off as an infirmary ward. Beneath this there
> is to be a room fitted up as a printing office, where some of the most
> intelligent lads are to be inducted into the mysteries of Caxton's
> craft.[14]

Bonner Road had been found, equipped and brought into use in a very short
time. Only the year before, international events had caused the public to direct
their sympathies and their money elsewhere. But even as the home was being
opened in London there was news of the offer of a farm in Lancashire. This
seemed the answer not only to the ever-growing needs to house children but
also to difficulties experienced with certain kinds of youngster. There were
boys who were thought 'affectionate and obedient' but who were ill at ease in
the cottage at Church Street. Their energies were too great to be confined and
they would abscond and be found elsewhere in the capital—at Smithfield
market, or assisting a drover with his cattle—or they might disappear
altogether. 'The reckless habits engendered by street life made it hard for
some lads to settle to ordinary life,' thought Stephenson.

Edgworth (as the new Home in Lancashire was to be called) would help that. It would give a change of locality, ample opportunity for pent-up energy to be expended, an offer of an open and healthy environment in which to grow. Edgworth had been offered the previous year by its owner, James Barlow. The new premises consisted of an inn, outbuildings and land. Barlow saw his gift as having two uses—an expansion of the Home's good work and one less place for Sunday drinking, cockfighting and dogfighting to take place. In 1872 Mager, Horner and Stephenson accompanied Barlow and his son, John R. Barlow, to the somewhat isolated moorland site.

Mager wrote of a hike across the moors, against a fierce wind. First they passed what was to him a misnamed little farmstead called 'Pleasant View', and further up, around the shoulder of the hill, in the midst of a 'wild and desolate' scene they came to the public house and its dilapidated barn 'standing grimly alone by the unfrequented farmhouse'.

The Edgworth project brought the work to a wider audience. Public meetings were held in Bolton and Manchester to raise £1200 to stock the farm and convert the property. By April Mr and Mrs Mager were installed as governor and matron.

The prospects of new kinds of training and a new kind of life at Edgworth met a need for some of the children that London had failed to do. But even now a new problem was to present itself. What were the youngsters to do when they got older? What useful work, what way of life, would be available to them then? How would they have the opportunity to practise the virtues of thrift and industriousness which the Home sought to instil in them? Where could they live that 'Christian life'? As the Magers prepared to leave London, new ideas were in the air. These would involve the Home looking much further afield than even the moors of Lancashire.

3 | Wide, open spaces: children as emigrants

In June 1872, Stephenson set sail for Canada on the steamship *Scotia*. He departed in a more sceptical frame of mind than the committee minutes of only three months before might have suggested. On 11 March the clerk had recorded:

> The Canadian project was discussed. A House of Reception would be necessary, and a Resident Officer to undertake the oversight of the children. It is considered highly desirable to initiate proceedings while Dr [Morley] Punshon [a notable preacher then living in Canada, an early influence on Stephenson and a helper and benefactor in the Canadian venture] was there, and accordingly the following resolution was agreed to: That having respect to the future destination of the children educated in this Home, and having received a communication from the Rev W.M. Punshon referring to the probable openings in Canada for the employment of such children, and inviting Mr Stephenson to visit Canada this spring in the interests of the Home; this Committee respectfully request the President of the Conference to sanction such arrangements as shall relieve Mr Stephenson for a few weeks from his circuit duties, for the purpose of his proceeding to Canada to establish in conjunction with Mr Punshon, a Canadian Branch of the Home.[1]

But for Stephenson the questions were: was it desirable to send children, and, if so, how many of them, to Canada? How were they to be chosen and transported? What help might be expected from Canada to secure the enterprise's success?

Stephenson in Canada

The president of the Methodist Conference, the Rev. Luke Wiseman, together with his son, joined Stephenson on the voyage. After visiting the USA they travelled to Canada. Arriving in Hamilton, the party met W.E. Sanford, who was to become treasurer of the Canadian branch. He was a senator and thus someone of influence within the Canadian government on the Home's behalf.

In search of answers to his questions Stephenson consulted local clergy, municipal officials, philanthropists, working men and employers. He also had lengthy interviews in Montreal with Ellen Bilborough and Miss Barber, who ran the receiving homes for emigrant children which had been established by Annie MacPherson. She was a well-known evangelical who had taken out her first party of children from England in 1869, thereafter taking out parties almost annually.[2]

What attracted Stephenson to Canada was the 'remarkably moral' tone of the country, the general influence of religion, plentiful work, and his belief that anyone prepared to be diligent would not go without. There was no feeling of 'caste' in the country, he reported. Like MacPherson and Barnardo, Stephenson emphasized the equality in Canadian households where food and tables were shared between the farmers and their young wards. However, the truth is that 'home children' were often stigmatized.

Canadian attitudes to such a scheme as Stephenson's were summed up in his belief that:

> *They do not wish to have the dregs of our pauper population cast into the midst of them, and they deprecate the sending of untrained children into their country; but they hail the idea of well trained children coming to them, and I was assured on all hands that the only difficulty we should find would be in supplying the applicants who would ask for our children.*[3]

His statement about opposition to untrained children implied the direction which the Home's policy would take. But before that, Stephenson came to an important decision so far as the Home's responsibilities were concerned: 'There is no person or body of persons in Canada who could do this work in the way we should wish to have it done. And we have the peculiar advantages for doing it. The reception which I met with amongst the ministers in Canada assures us of their cordial co-operation.'[4] This is perhaps not surprising: child emigration was frequently welcomed as a form of cheap labour.

The sending of children to Canada by the Home came not long after the modern pioneers of child migration—Maria Rye in 1868 and Annie MacPherson in 1869—had set about their work. The Home's policies preceded the (now) much more publicized and extensive work of Thomas Barnardo by eight years. (Barnardo had first entrusted some of his boys whom he considered would not be able to prosper at home to Annie Mac-Pherson and continued to use her organization to send children overseas until he took it over in 1904. Indeed, when Barnardo started his venture in 1882 the Home made the Hamilton house available to him until he could find quarters of his own.) But this was the emigration of modern times. The first child migrants had been settled in Richmond, Virginia, in 1618. And while the numbers from then until 1868 were comparatively small, thanks to the efforts of governments, boards of guardians, and philanthropists the belief in emigration as a solution had been a potent force within child care for two centuries. All too often the solution was less one of meeting the needs of the children, and more one of dispensing with those causing problems and whose upkeep was costly.

In the 1860s Canada had come to be seen as the ideal place to send British children: wide open spaces, the healthy farm life, the need for farm workers. (Stephenson himself had seen that vacancies for clerks and shop work were met by native labour). In an increasingly crowded island, with unimpeded urbanization visiting upon it various ills, the pastoral life, already deeply rooted in some aspects of English thought, had a persuasive power.

There could be no more dramatic and vivid expression of the idea of 'rescue', to which the philanthropic societies were devoted, than that children should be taken from the dangerous, corrupting streets to the rural life of the prosperous and expanding dominion. There was also a need, in the apogee of empire, to build up British, Anglo-Saxon stock, combined with the less elevated wish to meet the demands for cheap labour. More particularly, Ontario, where the Home was to establish its branch and, for the most part, settle its children, was conscious of Catholic expansion in nearby Quebec Province and thus looked kindly upon an influx of young Protestants.

The 'solution' of emigration

The Home, in its first years, had come across children whom it believed it would find difficult to settle in its premises in the urban areas where they had been found. Even at the opening ceremony of Bonner Road on 4 October 1871 there was news of the Lancashire farm, which was to become the home at Edgworth. But the potential numbers of children who would benefit from a rural home seemed likely to outweigh seriously the availability of such places.

Twenty years after Stephenson's seal of approval had been set upon the venture, Mager reiterated the reasons which impelled the policy: sending children to farms would militate against 'their lapse into former modes of living': there was to be had the 'health of body, and wholesome living; contentment, freedom and the rewards of honourable toil'.[5] But it had not been enough simply to remove children from England; urban life, wherever lived, had its perils. As Mager added:

> *The town-bred youth in his teens—the flabby, discontented, restless juvenile product of pavement and poverty must be weaned from the glare and the glitter, the vice and the unwholesome excitement of our streets. His habits must be steadied and renovated by a course of systematic industry, upon the land, if possible, miles from 'the madding crowd's ignoble strife'.[5]*

Stephenson had also seen emigration as the solution for children from certain types of background, for those whose 'parents showed only a sort of unintelligent and almost animal affection which thinks nothing and is prepared to sacrifice nothing for the permanent welfare of the child'.[6] But economic considerations also had their part to play. Alfred Mager estimated that keeping a little girl of four of five years of age in an institution in England might cost £50 to £200, or enough, as he put it, 'to save and bless half a dozen such little ones' through emigration. However, there were exceptions. Older girls of 'good character, antecedents and parentage' did not need to be sent abroad, for plenty of openings could be found for them in England. Such girls were 'respectable' and 'untrammeled by undesirable relatives'. Indeed, Mager went on to say, they might be in greater danger in Canada because of isolated dwellings and 'the pastoral pursuits in which they may be called to take part'.[7]

Before the first children from the Home arrived in Canada, Stephenson had shaped a policy which would, he hoped, place the Home above the criticisms and reservations of the Canadians to which he had referred in his report. Each child would be carefully chosen and would go with the consent—'in unmistakable written, signed and attested terms', as Mager had recommended[8]—of the parent or guardian. Their moral or physical fitness for the new life would be assured, and they would be trained. The Hamilton home, purchased by voluntary donations both in that town ($3,000) and Montreal

($1,500) and furnished with further donations of $2,000 from Montreal, would be both the reception and distribution centre and the home and office of the governor. The latter would oversee the approval of applicants, who far outnumbered the children available.

Almost all the emigrant societies—and in the peak years of 1870–1925 there were at least twenty-five of them—had separate stages of settling their children. The Home termed its stages 'adoption'; 'raising', which was less than adoption and where children lived as members of a family and undertook light chores; and 'service' or paid employment in a house, farm or shop.[9]

Placements

The Home was, from the very beginning, anxious to see that placements were properly monitored and inspected by its staff. It was another duty which fell to the governor. This was probably more easily said than done, for all the Home's good intentions. There would have been considerable difficulty in monitoring widely scattered settlements and children who might have been afraid to complain. The children also might look physically robust—the work would have been gruelling, the hours long—but many would have been traumatized by separation from family, friends and familiar surroundings.

Stephenson had persuaded the federal government to make a grant of $2 a head for each child brought to Canada, which was seen as approval by the government of its policy of emigration,[10] but there federal responsibility ended. None of the societies was bound by any official rules and regulations. Stephenson saw the governors' role in almost literally paternal terms. They, he said, must be 'thoroughly intelligent and judicious men', a 'sort of foster-father to the children in Canada during the whole period of their minority'.[11]

When Stephenson returned to England, he left behind him a committee to purchase a property and sort out details of its management. A year after Stephenson's exploratory journey, Francis Horner left Liverpool on the ocean-going streamer 'Polynesia' with the first party of forty-nine children.[12] They were among nearly 2,000 emigrants aboard, drawn from every European country. So large was the passenger list that the liner's cargo space had been converted, with sacrifice of comfort, into living quarters. With no deadweight, the journey was, at times, a rough one, with the ship's bows dipping in the sea and flooding on the forward deck.

The party arrived at Port Levy on 23 May 1873, eight days after embarking, and was met by the Rev. J.A. Allan, the town's Wesleyan minister and a Mr Haig, an agent representing the province of Ontario.

Their onward journey by train was no more comfortable than that by sea. Horner complained of 'a first class car of second rate quality' for 'a most wearisome journey over the most horrible railroad in existence...' At Toronto they missed the last train to Hamilton and bedded down, under rugs and on a bare floor, in the emigrant sheds.

But when they reached the Hamilton home the journey must have seemed worthwhile. The house was approached by a curved drive, several hundred yards long, bordered by grass and much arable land. A large lawn, with flower beds, stretched in front of the house. To the left there was an orchard and at the back the gardener had a cottage. The two-storey building had a large verandah and a balcony running its whole width. Few provisions had been organized or furniture provided and the boards were bare but the rooms were light, large and airy.

Two hundred applications had been received for the children and a committee was established to deal with them. After Stephenson went with a party the following year he explained the method of selecting new homes for the children.

A notice was inserted in one or two newspapers to advertise the arrival of a party; then every applicant was sent a questionnaire, the answers to which gave an idea of the applicant's status and character and the kind of child he was looking for. The application had to be accompanied by a character reference from a clergyman or magistrate, and preference was given to Christians. The child's character and fitness for the situation were then matched to the application.

By August, Horner could report of his party that only nine of the original forty-nine children were left: twenty-six had gone to farms, some of them having been farm children in England. In addition to board and lodgings, some of them received as much as $6 (24 s) a month (but some only half this sum). Two boys went to learn carpentry and two to blacksmith's and wheelwright's trades, and two more went to the Methodist Book Room to learn printing. Mr Sanford's warehouse took two more. Of the fifteen girls, five were adopted by 'Christian families', six engaged as domestic servants, and four had gone to farming families. The girls placed as servants were to receive $3 a month. Wage earners had their savings remitted to a specially opened savings account. Quarterly reports were submitted to the Hamilton committee on the children's health and conduct, and these reports were then sent to England.

Although Horner had found some prejudice against such children coming to Canada, John Pope, the Minister for Agriculture and Immigration, promised increased financial assistance for the next party. The ministry also gave the Home's agent a free, country-wide rail pass.

A few of the children were eventually returned to England: one boy was said to be hopeless and indifferent, complaining of overwork (which might not have been without justification). One girl went back to England in disgrace—she was dishonest and it was felt she had damaged the Home's good reputation. The children often wrote to Stephenson.[13] Possibly they had been encouraged to do so in gratitude for the new life which he had arranged for them. The head of Home would have been for them a link with the past. One said:

> I am so much disappointed at not hearing from you. I can hardly write again. You don't know how I feel when week after week passes and no letter comes for me. But I have been having my likeness taken, and I thought that if I sent you one that would perhaps get you to write. But I know you are so busy, it is hard to find time. You will be very pleased to hear that I have joined Class, and am trying to love God and do right. I am going to stay here until the Spring; I like it better than the farm I was at. I get to Church much oftener. Your loving child.

By contrast another was more formal: 'Dear Sir, I think the time has arrived once more for me to send a few items of intelligence.' Another signed off 'your true friend'.

The children's stays in the homes which took them were sometimes less permanent than might have been wished. J.J. Kelso, secretary of Neglected and Dependent Children in Ontario, observed:

> Children are frequently changed from one home to another, but this cannot be regarded as evidence of unfitness, as the arrangements are usually for one year, and the management believes in making changes if better terms or kinder treatment can be secured thereby.[14]

But even 'frequent changes' for these periods and these reasons would have been unsettling to any child, let alone one an ocean away from home.

But whatever any initial problems of settling the children, they seem not to have dented either the Home's enthusiasm or that of its supporters for the scheme. By May 1874 *The Children's Advocate* could reveal that $6,000 had already been subscribed in Canada for the project with the hope of another

$4,000 by the end of the year. A four-point plan was drawn up. This would involve a party of thirty-nine boys to go out in April the following year. They would be accompanied by Mr and Mrs Tiley who would take charge of the home, keeping six boys to maintain the grounds and accommodation. The existing barns and outbuildings at Hamilton would be converted to take up to fifty boys, and the principal would visit Hamilton with a large party of boys and girls who would already be trained in Canada, though where and how was not stated.

Criticisms of emigration

However enlightened policies of the Home might have been by the standards of the time, as early as 1877 there was general criticism in England of child emigration as 'inhuman', exposing children to 'great disadvantages and to much obloquy'.[15] But the most important criticism was of the 'total absence of efficient supervision which exposed the children to suffering and wrong, for which they found neither relief nor redress'. This last quotation came from the report by Andrew Doyle,[16] a barrister and civil servant, whose inquiry had been set up by the Government to investigate disquiet. He had concentrated specifically on the work of Maria Rye and Annie MacPherson who sent children largely in co-operation with boards of guardians (though Barnardo's made use of MacPherson's agency). He found their selection of children, reception, selection of applicants, inspection and aftercare grossly wanting. The report commented:

> *To send them as emigrants can be regarded not as a way of improving their position, but simply getting rid of them at a cheap rate ... If they be reasonably well prepared for service, it is difficult to understand why they would be sent out of the country in which one hears from every household complaints of a dearth of domestic servants and of the want of young hands in various branches of industry.*

For the most part Doyle's report was ignored: the supporters of Canadian emigration, who would have included the boards of guardians who saw emigration as a means of relieving the Poor Rate burden, lobbied in the Commons. Also, fears of increasing central government control, which were implied in his recommendations, undermined any support that the report might have had in Canada itself.

But at the same time as Doyle was reporting, a delegation from the Home was presenting a memorial to Mr Letellier de St Just, the Canadian Minister for Immigration, seeking financial help on grounds that would have found favour with Doyle: the Home wanted to improve its training both for farm work and other trades and to provide a superintendent at the Hamilton branch. The Home's committee said that they were 'exceedingly gratified to find that, with scarcely any exception, the boys and girls already sent out are doing well, and giving great satisfaction to their employers.' This request led to the payment of $2 a head bonus for each child, other than workhouse children, brought to Canada. This not only assisted the Home but encouraged emigration policies generally.[17] In its own rebuttal of criticism of the principle of emigration, the Home said that Canada was a loyal dominion with a great future, prosperity, good rail and road links, few public houses but many churches, and easily obtainable and well-paid agricultural employment.[18]

In the 1880s emigration was buoyant. Following a depression and in the wake of the Doyle report, restrictions imposed on passes between the provinces of Ontario and Quebec, limiting the movement of workers, led to an even greater demand for farm workers and domestic help. But despite pressure from farmers and others for a steady flow of labour, the Home refused to slacken its policies: care in the selection of children and their potential homes and employers continued. Such a policy meant that Frank Hills, appointed governor in 1894, could report that the Home was considered first among all the bodies operating a child migration scheme. But by that time, the Canadian branch was concerned that its work was becoming more difficult year by year.[19] There was a general industrial depression throughout North America which made for antipathy toward any form of immigration but especially that of adolescent boys who were seen to be taking men's jobs. According to the branch's report of 1893–94:

> *The consequences of this state of feeling amongst large bodies of the people, is that immigration of children is not judged upon a calm consideration of its merits, but with prejudice and feeling. If an immigrant lad misbehaves himself, he is not judged as a Canadian boy would be. If, unhappily, one of them should be charged with any public offence, the case is reported and commented upon in the newspapers much more eagerly and extensively than if the young criminal were native-born. In fact, an atmosphere of prejudice surrounds all immigration work, instead of the sympathy which formerly existed.*

Moreover, the work was not assisted by the fact that more and more organizations were sending out children to Canada, thus decreasing the number of applicants coming forward for the Home's children. Nonetheless, as the Home's emigration work was comparatively small and the children carefully selected, there was, said the report, little difficulty in finding suitable placements. When the depression had passed, the Home, it believed, could look forward to 'brighter' prospects.

The work did continue and although the Home had nothing to fear from official policies being strengthened, those policies remained lax: it would not be until 1924 that the immigration of children below working age would be banned in Canada.[20] But by then the great wave of emigration had long since passed. In 1896 a total of 3,015 children came to Canada under the combined aegis of all the societies; at the turn of the century the number had fallen to 977. With the coming of the Great War all emigration was suspended because of the dangers of submarine action. After the war, the potential numbers of emigrant children had increased greatly but so had the costs and the Home opened an Emigration Fund, quoting the figure of £10 to pay for each child's passage and initial settlement.

By the 1930s, when Britain was in the grip of an economic recession, 4,000 children had passed through the Hamilton branch. Compared with the total number of children who were sent to Canada, this was not great: in 1883–89, 2,000 children a year were being sent to the Dominion by all agencies.[21] In 1934 1,078 Main Street, Hamilton, was closed. John H. Litten, by that time the Home's principal, reported that for the past five or six years restrictions on emigration operated by the federal government had prevented children from being sent out and the branch's work had, as a consequence, been brought 'to a standstill'. Moreover, the surroundings of the branch were no longer suitable for its purposes: over the decades the town had encroached on the calm peacefulness of the house and grounds. The property, Litten recorded, had been sold.[22]

Australia

As Canada became less attractive, so Australia beckoned. Shortly before the Second World War a group of boys from various branches of the Home had been sent there under the auspices of that country's Northcote Farm Schools.[23] The coming of war and the expansion of the Home seems to have delayed the Home's involvement. The pre-war child emigration (which had also been under the auspices of the Fairbridge Farm Schools and the Catholic

Order of the Christian Brothers) had been assisted by government grants. With the war over, the Australian government adopted a vigorous policy to encourage immigration, including that of children. Again, as with Canada, there were less than noble motives at work. Australia adopted a 'white Australia' immigration policy and feared that its closeness to non-white Asian countries would threaten its Anglo-Saxon (itself originally immigrant) stock.

In 1946 the Australian government passed the Immigration (Guardianship of Children) Act laying down regulations and giving responsibility in each state to a director of child welfare who would have to ensure the children's accommodation, placement in employment and welfare up to the age of twenty-one. The next year the government announced it was looking for 50,000 children, mainly from the UK and Europe.

The perceived success of the pre-war venture led Litten, at the request of the Home's general committee, to visit Australia in 1948 to look more closely at the prospects for further emigration. His report was enthusiastic about the prospects and opportunities; the Australian government would meet all travel costs and give a grant toward the cost of equipping the Home's establishments.[24]

In its negotiations with the government, the Home laid down a seven-point plan. This would ensure that religion would be recognized as the basis of the children's education and upbringing, while every endeavour would be made to create a normal family life by having children in groups of eight to ten, wherever possible of boys and girls. Efforts would be made to ensure that the children would grow up under the guidance of adults who would stay with them, so that they would enjoy stability. The houses where the children would live would be well built, substantial, comfortable, and homely, with modern labour-saving devices. Experts would be called upon to look at the children's individual aptitudes and needs, and to find them occupations to which they would be best suited. Last, staff would receive adequate training.[25] Litten was also influenced by a friend, who held a senior position with the Fairbridge Farm Schools.[26]

When Litten returned he was in favour of taking up an offer of the Methodist Children's Home in Melbourne. It offered fifty places to an equal number of boys and girls, aged four to ten. Litten was looking to the longer-term prospect of sending teenagers to whom (it was believed) Australia would give a new start. But whatever his hopes, they were not unanimously shared by the Home's executive committee. The proposal was to send an explanatory letter to all parents and guardians of the Home's children to ascertain their willingness for the children to be considered for the scheme. An application form would be attached to the letters. The plan for the first year was to send three parties of fifty children accompanied by four Sisters, the women workers whom Stephenson had by now recruited, who felt a sense of vocation for the work (see chapter 4).

Some members of the executive felt that the Home was rushing too quickly into the scheme. What was the experience of children who had gone? In a private note to Litten, John Waterhouse, by this time principal-designate, made known his own reservations. He echoed the concerns of C.F. Walpole, the general secretary, T.O. Buck, the financial secretary, and Alan Jacka, the education secretary. This opposition may have considerably dampened enthusiasm and prevented the Home from becoming more heavily involved. As it was, from 1950 to 1954 it sent only ninety-one children to Australia compared with the national figure of 2,324 between 1945 and 1955.[27]

In 1950 the venture was under way. There is no record of how children were selected or what the response was from parents to the initial letter. But Home Office regulations (which the Home seems to have abided by) stipulated that selection should be with the help of trained social workers and have regard to physical and mental health, social history, school record, home visits, relatives and an interview with the child to ensure that it had a reasonable understanding of what going to another country on such a basis would mean. There also had to be specific preparation in this country for life in the new one. One Sister who went to Australia has said that the preparation opened up many old wounds as some children were been made aware of the reasons why they were in care. Others wanted to see their parents before deciding to go and were shocked by the conditions in which they lived and the apparent lack of parental interest in them.[28]

All children who were nominated were gathered together at Stokehurst House, Alverstoke, for a month to be prepared for their departure.[29] Fifty-three boys and twenty-nine girls went in the first year. To each of the four places where they were settled—Sydney, Adelaide, Melbourne and Perth—went a Sister from the UK. By this time Litten had retired and the Home's *Year Book* could report that, living near Sydney himself, he could keep a watchful eye on the developments which he had set in motion.

From available records the Home's policy seems to have been undertaken with sensitivity and—given the dissent within the executive—some gravity. However, one researcher has found two areas for criticism. The first is that the explanatory letter to parents stated: 'It is, of course, hoped that those who travel to Australia will stay there a reasonable time, but arrangements are made to bring back to this country any who do not fit happily into their new surroundings.' However, while some unhappy children did write to their parents asking to be able to return, they did not. When parents approached the Home, they found that the children could only come back if the parents were able to foot the bill for the return passage, which was £65. This was beyond the means of most parents.

The second area of criticism is that while the children had lost or been separated from their parents, seventeen of the ninety-one were also separated from brothers or sisters with whom they had been living in children's homes in the UK.[30]

Child migration continued into the 1950s, though the Home appears to have been the least enthusiastic of its proponents.[31] The dissent in the executive had dented any possibility of a large-scale involvement from the beginning and perhaps Waterhouse's succeeding of Litten dealt the final blow. Anyway, emigration had never been a policy for the majority of children deprived, for whatever reason, of the care of their natural parents. Also, increasingly, even for the minority for whom it had been felt to be suitable, other forms of care were seen to be preferable to taking very vulnerable children to new lives on the other side of the world.

The criticisms of the Doyle report, more than eighty years before, had never been applicable to the work of the Home: indeed, it had been a pioneer in ensuring that suitable staff were appointed and trained, children properly selected and satisfactory homes found for them. It would, though, be unrealistic to believe that these ideals were always met, given (by today's standards) the rudimentary checks that could be made, the vastness of the countries to which the children were sent, and the isolated areas in which they often found themselves. There was also the stigma which attached to being a 'home child'. And yet there were children—sent by other societies, as well as the Home—who did find material success and personal happiness in their adopted countries. But public opinion and public policy was changing and the Home responded to it, as it had when Stephenson, accepting the feelings of the times in which he lived, had believed transatlantic rescue to be of value.

4 Onward, Christian soldiers: towards the National Children's Home

If there was a spirit of adventure in going to the desolate Lancashire moors to create what would become Edgworth, the first of the Home's establishments away from London, it was not how Alfred Mager first saw it. On 17 April 1872, he and his wife, twenty-four boys, four girls and a small group of helpers found themselves in an inhospitable environment. Mager wrote of 'dirt and desolation; barren bog and dreary moss, stretching out before our gaze'.[1]

Wheatsheaf Farm was a wayside inn, a tall, solid brick-built place, with a dilapidated barn. It had been a place for Sunday drinking, cockfighting and dogfighting, out of the way of the police. When it came on the market, James Barlow bought it, with a double intention: to do away with a den of iniquity and to provide a new property for the Home. But that new home had to be created, literally, by the hands of Mager and his party. First of all, to provide drinking water, a reservoir was created by staff and boys. Then the boys did all the work in constructing the new building: replacing windows, doors and stairs in the old inn; draining the bogs; removing boulders so large that they had to be cut with wedges driven in by hammers and rolled by hands on planks. In the face of what was being done, Mager's earlier reservations gave way to a new optimism. He wrote:

> No better sphere of industrial training could have been found for rough street lads, or even for weakly orphans upon this industrial moorland estate. From the crowded streets to the fields; from the squalid court and the filthy alley to the bracing hillside, where pure streams gurgle, and the sweet air stirs, is a translation that gives vigour to weaklings; while for moral reformation the change is equally helpful and salutary.[2]

But such translation was not universally welcomed. For one thing local people were not happy about such children coming into their midst. Some of the children themselves, brought up in the hubbub of the city, disliked the quietness and the cold winds which blew over the moors. There was occasional violence: one boy tried to throw a stone from a roof onto a member of the staff and missed, but another boy did severely cut the head of the labour master. That the new home and regime was not entirely to the children's tastes can be seen from the fact that, on another occasion, twenty boys mutinied, arming themselves with pointed sticks and leather straps. They defied and terrorized the staff and the rebellion was only quelled upon Mager's return.[3]

Mager had referred to 'weakly' children. Edgworth had been intended for delicate children (though it was never restricted to them) in the then common belief that a rural life and fresh air was the best remedy. Likewise, for children whose moral welfare was threatened by all the vices which the city could offer, Edgworth also tallied with the idea of rescuing them from urban perils.

Only three years after its foundation, the Home's foray into Lancashire turned it into a national organization. For its fourth establishment, it also moved away from London: in 1875 the industrial school at Gravesend was founded. The development of these schools was intended for children under the age of fourteen committed by the courts for truancy, petty theft, vagrancy and begging and in need of care but beyond the control of their parents (where they had any).

The pace of the Home's development was such that in 1873 the Wesleyan Methodist Conference took a decision of far-reaching consequences for Stephenson and the Home. He explained events in a letter to his wife:

> I am glad to tell you that the Conference appointed me yesterday Principal of the Children's Home, with unanimity, and without a syllable of opposition, or even a question. Everybody blesses the work and congratulates me … The Conference received my Report, and spent near an hour and a half in conversation upon it. [Several members] spoke most kindly in support of the work. In fact, it has taken deep hold of the Methodist heart, and is counted fairly among the institutions of the Church.
>
> This is a most blessed Conference. The spirit of unity and power is given to us as I have never known it before. Surely we are on the eve of good days.[4]

And indeed, they were, if only with a comparatively minor disappointment. The committee determined upon a new venture: a training ship. A fund-raising group was formed, an inaugural meeting held at the Mansion House, sums of money were promised and the government offered to furnish the vessel, but the plan proved abortive. Sufficient money was not forthcoming, yet it was money that was needed to bolster what was already in existence—there was an accumulating debt on Bonner Road. While Stephenson was away in Canada in 1874, the committee decided to buy the freehold of Bonner Road, which by now had grown to nearly a dozen houses, and start an appeal for £10,000. This was achieved but the expansion of the Home continued to incur debt to the extent that in 1876 it was said that £10,000 was needed to free the Home of its liabilities[5]. The committee then took a decision that there would be no further expansion until it was free of debt or all the money for new branches could be secured.

Boarding out and adoption

While the impetus of the Home was to be overwhelmingly the provision of residential care for much of its first century, it did board out children, as fostering was then known. Adoption was not made legal until 1926. Although the annual report for 1891–92 records twenty-five children as 'adopted'[6], these would have been informal arrangements, in the absence of any legal arrangements closer to the long-term fostering of today. In the 1860s a group of influential women had come together to lobby for boarding out (their work was later to grow into the National Committee for Promoting Boarding Out of Pauper Children). Florence Davenport Hill's book, *Children of the State*, published in 1868, pointed to the damaging effects—especially for girls—of institutional care. But the National Committee also saw boarding out as a means by which girls could be trained and thus create a larger supply of labour, particularly for domestic service.[7]

Despite initial distrust by Poor Law institutions, boarding out came to be seen as an alternative to residential care from the middle of the 1880s, so that by 1887 eleven per cent of children in the care of the Poor Law were boarded out.[8] The voluntary bodies were slower to accept boarding out. One of the advantages of the residential care which they offered was for children not to be in the care of the Poor Law.[9] There is no mention in the Home's annual reports of boarding out until 1908, when it is stated that the practice had been going on since the 1880s. In Birmingham boarding out was started in 1905 when it was noted that 'in consequence of the congested condition of the Home, the principal [of the local establishment, not Stephenson] received sanction of the committee to the boarding out of ten of the smaller children in suitable homes'.[10]

Within four years a quarter of the National Children's Home's children were being cared for in the same manner, but this rate was not to be reached again until 1930, after which there was a rapid falling away in the numbers being fostered. In 1939 only about 200 (or 7 per cent) of the Home's children were being fostered.[11] In his book *A History of Child Care*, Roy Parker suggests that the Home's sluggishness, compared with other voluntary agencies, may have been due to the fact that the 'strong missionary flavour' of its work accounted for a particular emphasis on residential care: the homes were communities where children could grow up in a religious atmosphere and missionary workers trained.[12]

There may be an element of truth in this but Stephenson was not alone in his missionary purpose: the Waifs and Strays also had a religious basis, while Barnardo himself was much more zealous and evangelistic than his Methodist counterpart. It is also the case that, with the turn of the century, and certainly after the First War, a more secular society came into being, and the voluntary agencies were less prone to talk in the same evangelistic tones as had the early pioneers.

In line with other agencies, the Home called back boarded out children to its homes when they left school. It was, though, stricter than others in this. The rule was that 'they should come into one of the Branches of the Home when 7 or 8 years of age.'[13] Why this policy was imposed on children at such an early age is not known. Parker says the belief that it was to do with missionary zeal falls down when one considers the large-scale emigration of children to Canada which the Home was then organizing. Sending them across the Atlantic Ocean into the care of Canadian families in remote places could only weaken considerably the influence which the Home could exert over them[14] (see chapter 3).

When some of the foster-parents became so attached to their children that they were reluctant to be parted from them, they 'adopted' them. Adoption, unofficial though it was, is recorded early on in the Home's life, families being 'approved' for the purpose. In 1891 twenty-five children had been adopted, including several with a sibling like the 'little brother and sister ... adopted by a worthy couple'; and 'a girl rescued from gross cruelty and neglect in a northern town ... and adopted by a minister and his wife'.[15] Older children, too, were adopted, as was the boy in the 1890s of whom it was said, 'the child shows propensity to vice—associates with bad lads, plays truant when sent to school and is a constant anxiety.'[16] By 1920, 260 children had been 'adopted'.[17]

Expansion

While Stephenson had been slow to recognize the case for boarding out, he was progressive in other ways. He had founded a 'cripples' parlour', a form of day care. In 1895 he was concerned about the situation of children with epilepsy and longing for 'a little house where a dozen such sufferers could be properly tended'.[18] Hope House for girls was founded in London, while boys with epilepsy went to Gravesend when the industrial school moved to Farnborough.

But whatever the progress of boarding out, it was residential care which continued to form the main thrust of the Home's work. In 1880 a branch at Ramsey, Isle of Man, opened as a result of the donation of a property. A wealthy Methodist, Solomon Jevons, had for some while wanted to assist a new development by the foundation of an orphanage for the children of Christian, and especially Methodist, parents. This was a new departure for the Home, for until then it had never considered itself to be concerned exclusively with children from any one denomination, or indeed of any at all.

Jevons would donate £9,000 (in addition to the £1,000 he was already giving to the Thanksgiving Fund, set up to celebrate the admission of lay people to membership of the Conference in 1877) if the Church would put in £10,000 match it. The orphanage (it was the first time that the Home had used the word to describe one of its ventures, 'refuge' being the common term) was to be situated at New Oscott, Sutton Coldfield, near Birmingham. It was to be named after Princess Alice, daughter of Queen Victoria, who had died through kissing one of her children who was suffering from diphtheria, a story calculated to appeal to the mawkish aspect of the Victorians. The foundation stone was laid in 1882 and by 1906 nine houses and additional school premises had been built. Eventually farm lands, a laundry and a bakery were added to make it more or less self-sufficient. In 1887 came the home at Alverstoke, Hampshire.

It had been decided that the Church's Thanksgiving Fund would give £5,000 to the Home, of which £4,500 went to meet its debt. But it soon became clear, with the success of fund-raising, that the Home would have considerably more than the £500 surplus to hand. So with this Stephenson arranged for an extension to Bonner Road, which would include the chapel which he had always wanted, above which would be a schoolroom. With the chapel, the choir could come into its own. Stephenson was noted for his own fine voice and the choir was very close to his heart. It was an integral part of the Home's life and mission, and would go on tours up and down the country; it continued to do so well into the present century.

Stephenson saw the choir very much as a part of his ministry. Missions and meetings, often in the open air, were held round about Bonner Road and elsewhere, at which he preached and the choir sang. The Home also had a fife and drum band, which would take part in these events. On Temperance Sunday there was a great procession from the gates of Bonner Road, when children and staff, band and choir, and members of East End temperance societies marched off. Stephenson was at the head of the procession, accompanied by 'Black Bob', a notorious local drunkard, converted and reformed, swinging the leg of a brass bedstead that stood in for a mace. Here was the living and sober proof that no one was beyond redemption.

The Home's work had projected Stephenson to a national prominence in the Methodist Church. He served on various of its committees but was never drawn only to child care or welfare matters. He was one of the leaders of the movement which eventually secured the admission of lay people (or laymen, as was then effectively the case) as members of the Conference, thus breaking the monopoly of the clergy as decision makers. In 1890 he became President of the Conference, leading the UK delegation to the Methodist Ecumenical Conference in Washington.

Despite his being 'set aside' by Conference as principal of the Home, he continued his pastoral role as a minister, though his circuits were in London and near to his work for the Home. When he had first come to London he had been elected to the London School Board for Bethnal Green. In 1893 he became a member of the Mansion House Committee on Distress in London and four years later a member of the Committee of the Prince of Wales's Hospital Fund (later the King Edward's Hospital Fund for London, now the King's Fund).

All this took its toll on Stephenson. Ill health had prevented him being present when the foundation stone for Princess Alice Orphanage was laid in 1882. He was on a ten-month tour of South Africa, Australasia, the Pacific, and the United States, a convalescence to restore his health. According to Bradfield, his biographer, the work for the Thanksgiving Fund, of which he had been one of its four general secretaries, had proved to be the final straw. He was 'exhausted in mind and body', and 'it became necessary that he should put a wide distance between himself and his ordinary anxieties.'[19] Progressive in some of his political views, Stephenson was, nevertheless, a man who reflected a popular view of his time, as his reflections on his year-long travels, undertaken with his wife and daughter, show. He wrote:

> *... it seems to me that to any thoughtful Englishman the British Empire is, next to the Christian religion, the greatest fact of these latter days. No man, who desires to measure at their true value the great social and moral forces which are making the world of the future, should neglect an opportunity to see that greater Britain which lies all round the globe, where men of our own blood, our own speech, and our own religion, are reproducing this dear old England, with a freedom and elasticity which is not possible to us at home.*
>
> *... I believe that in the accomplishment of His great purposes the Anglo-Saxon race is, and is to be, the most potent factor.[20]*

In his absence the deteriorating state of the Home's finances had been exposed by the Rev. G. Bate, who had, with the committee's approval, taken charge. Even after the success of the Thanksgiving Fund appeal in paying off outstanding debt, as well as providing £10,000 toward the Princess Alice Orphanage, it had been discovered that there was still a considerable bank overdraft. Further investigation revealed there was a debt of £2,276, which, when other calculations had been done, rose to about £5,000. Money-saving strategies were adopted—all legacies were to be devoted to clearing the debt; economies introduced on everyday expenditure; and a thorough overhaul brought about of the Home's financial system—which resulted in the situation being righted and the possibility, again, of expansion, and improvements being made to existing homes.

Sisters of the children

Stephenson's poor health was caused by overwork. There were no half mea-sures for him: it was he who had taken the children to Canada, he who had toured with the choir, he who, freed from the circuit, continued to adopt a pastoral role away from the Home. The founding and life of the Sisterhood had been no exception. During the travels of his younger days, Stephenson had been much influenced by the work of Immanuel Wichen at the *Rauhe Haus*, near Hamburg. There children lived in small groups, in stark contrast to the prevalent institutional care common elsewhere. But for Stephenson there was one drawback. Writing in *The Children's Advocate* in 1871 he said that 'the motherly and sisterly influence is waning' and believed the influence of Christian women to be invaluable.[21] He also wrote:

> *One feature of our work is the employment to a very large extent of Christian women in the domestic management and moral training of children. Many institutions, as is inevitable, rely on women for the training of girls. Ours is the only one in which the training of boys in all routine and influences of domestic life is committed to women. And yet, is it not the right plan? What person is there who will not recognise that the best influence in his early life came from his mother? Of course, there are points in the discipline of our boys in which the presence and influence of men are necessary but in the quiet of the domestic circle, in all those influences which are expressed in the word 'home', the presence of women is of the highest importance . . .*
>
> *But I must again protest against the popular conception that any decent women will do such work as this. Therefore, it is a huge mistake to suppose that anybody who may have proved incompetent in any other walk of life, but who can wash a child's face or sew a button upon a child's dress, is fit for such work as ours.*[22]

In 1871, two years after Stephenson had visited Wichen, he had visited the battlefields of the Franco-Prussian War and had travelled as far as Vienna. This trip allowed him to visit Kaiserwerth to look at the hospital where there was progressive care of elderly people undertaken by the deaconesses, as part of the work of the Inner Mission. Here the guiding light was Pastor Theodore Fliedner, who had found his inspiration in the New Testament, where women had been set aside for work of service and for acceptance in the official ministry of the early church.

Kaiserwerth was a strong influence on the Deaconess Movement, which was made up of women who felt a sense of vocation for social (and, in some cases, evangelistic) work.. It was here that Florence Nightingale, enthused by the type of nursing she observed, had convinced her family that she should become a nurse.[23] Barnardo, in 1875, turned over his own family home to a home for his order of deaconesses and many of his future staff and co-workers were to come from the deaconesses of Mildmay Park, well known in evangelical circles.[24] In July of that same year, *The Children's Advocate* had carried an article about the work of the Kaiserwerth Deaconesses in establishing an orphanage in Syria. Stephenson seems also to have had some knowledge of, and been influenced by the work of, Lucy Rider Meyer who had begun deaconess work in Chicago.

And so, when it came to putting his words about the need for women in his work into practice, Stephenson had some idea of the form it might take. Much that he saw at Kaiserwerth determined the role that women would play within the Home. When the training department was established at Bonner Road— 'what is needed is a technical school of Christian labour'—it was specifically for men and women. But by the end of the 1870s mixed training had been abandoned, for reasons which one of the organization's historians finds obscure.[25] This may have been a lack of financial support from the committee, perhaps reluctant to train men who would be likely to enter the ordained ministry and thus be 'lost' to the Home. Whether or not this was coincidental, at the same time that mixed training was coming to an end, Stephenson brought in probationer Sisters.

At first these Sisters were 'old girls' of the Home who became 'Sisters of the Children'. Each day, they assisted in domestic tasks until 10 a.m., then engaged in outdoor exercise for an hour. From 11 a.m. to 1 p.m. various lessons were given by 'an educated lady' in a specially designated room. After this they met Stephenson for spiritual and intellectual instruction.[26] This 'on the job' training, together with a few lectures, was later to develop into correspondence courses in subjects like child care, Christian teaching, Bible study, English literature, principles of social work and housewifery. A certificate would be given to those who came through successfully.[27]

It was not many months after the foundation of the Sisterhood before Stephenson was moving away from training old girls and appealing to all Protestant women to join the work. Sisters were not to be hirelings nor be involved in the 'mere institutional aspect of the work'. They were encouraged to see the work as a vocation. Salaries were paid at less than might be expected elsewhere but were to be sufficient for everyday needs. 'Mental strength, good education, refined and gentle manners' and, above all, a deep religious faith, were seen as the virtues for such work.

A gift of £500 brought 7 Agnes Terrace for the Sisters, though they were later to move to 84 Bonner Road. The Sisterhood was beginning to take on a distinguishing form: Mewburn House opened in July 1890 with Sister Rita Hawkins and one probationer, who were joined three months later by three others. There was Biblical instruction but also training in child care, care of the sick, and home and foreign mission work. Uniforms were prescribed. Eight years later Willard House opened near Bonner Road as a training establishment for the Sisters. They not only ran the home themselves and underwent training but undertook placements in the Home's establishments. 'We have learned to be the servants of each other,' said Sister Ruth Northcroft, who was in charge, in language sounding increasingly like that of the Anglican and Catholic religious orders.

By 1892, 140 women were working as Sisters in various capacities, forty-seven of them Sisters of the Children. By the turn of the century lady associates, women in sympathy with the work but unable to take up full membership of the order, had been established and Sisters of the Children had become a separate part of the order.

Stephenson's commitment to his female staff established their standing within the organization; his work for the Sisterhood was to sustain it long after his death. The word 'ordination' was coined in 1936 but there was a gradual feeling developing thirty years later that 'recognition' was a word more suitable for the work of the Home, and 'ordination' for the Church. Sisters, too, were eventually all to become qualified child care workers, so that the two roles of Sister and child care worker became blurred, although being a Sister continued to have a vocational air about it. Uniforms came to be thought inappropriate (not least because it did nothing to encourage good dress sense in the girls in the Home's care).

In 1979 the official centenary was celebrated, though, of course, the embryo of the Sisterhood had come into being before that. But in 1985, with a steadily declining membership, the Sisterhood was closed down and its life marked by two services of thanksgiving at Stephenson Hall.[28]

Ellen Stephenson

Ellen Stephenson's later years were marked by ill health and increasing disability and in October 1890 she died. The marriage of Stephenson and his wife had been a long and happy one. She had not taken a leading role in the Home, but she had given her support. In the earliest years before the home for girls was open, she had taken a girl into their family home and cared for her. Certainly her own upbringing, with its emphasis on caring for others, giving freely of both time and money, had meant that she had not objected when her husband's life had taken the course that it had. But living in London had not been agreeable to her or to her health, and Stephenson's frequent absences from home 'were much against her wish'.[29] She would have preferred the life of an ordinary minister's wife on rural circuits, and she had done as best she could. She had for many years taken part in the management of a mother's meeting and had also conducted weekly religious services for the girls in the Home. Their daughter, Dora, was to become a Sister.

Stephenson did not have time to grieve: the work of the Home; his election that year as President of the Wesleyan (now Methodist) Conference, and the preparations for the Wesley centenary all took place that year. Although he had suffered with his own health in recent years, he was still a comparatively young man and in 1893 he married again. His new wife was Ella Macpherson, a Sister, who had worked in the Isle of Man branch. She herself had come into the care of the Home when she had been orphaned.

The appointment of a vice-principal

Stephenson's health continued to show no improvement. He took on more than he was able to deal with. In 1894 he accepted appointment as superintendent of the Victoria Park circuit, within which fell Bonner Road, and in the same year also became chairman of the First London District of the Church. This was no sinecure: it was the equivalent to the work of a bishop, overseeing the work of the circuits and ministers within the district. It proved too much.

He was released from the district position and, with Mrs Stephenson, visited Canada and the United States for a rest. But even there the cares of the Home obtruded. There was an accusation made that the home in Hamilton, Canada, which was a distribution centre for migrant children, was no more than a conduit for children from poor backgrounds in their own country to be dumped in the dominion. The charge was unfounded but Stephenson, on his 'rest', was drawn into the controversy and had to put pressure on the Canadian government to carry out an investigation which was to clear the Home's reputation.

In his absence, the committee decided that they would appoint a vice-principal and this they did in 1898 in the person of the Rev. Arthur Gregory, who had come into the Home's work, before entering the ministry, as a trainee in 1873. It was part of Stephenson's strategy to bring on young men like Gregory in the hope that they would continue in the service of the Home. How Stephenson reacted to Gregory's elevation so many years later is none too clear.

But however he felt, Stephenson returned from his transatlantic travels, maybe less refreshed than he had hoped. He came back to his work, to more financial problems resulting from heavy capital debts, and to the further extension of the Home's work. Within a month of his sixtieth birthday, he fell ill again, worn out, a man looking older than his years. He sought sun and rest in Italy, far beyond the reach of any of the Home's problems. Someone who saw him at Cannes said: 'He was still active, but his energy was ebbing. He shrank from company, except that of a few old friends.'[30] His sixtieth birthday was widely celebrated but five months later, in May 1900, his letter of resignation was read to the committee's annual meeting.

Cyril Davey, whose short biography of Stephenson [31] shows, at times, an imaginative gift, says that the principal found it difficult to accept the appointment of Gregory as vice-principal. It was not that Stephenson did not like Gregory or have faith in his abilities, but Stephenson's name and that of the Home had become synonymous. Stephenson's biographer, Bradfield, who knew both men and many of the principal persons associated with the Home, makes no mention of any dissent about the appointment. However, when Stephenson did resign, the scholarly John Pendlebury, whom Stephenson had appointed deputy governor of the London branch of the Home many years before, wrote to him, in a rather hurried style:

> *Your letter [of resignation] brings me a message which causes me the keenest and most sincere grief. I am wondering what can [be] the occasion of your taking this sad step. I am wondering whether the condition of your health, or unhappiness caused to you in any way and by me or by any of us, is the cause. Perhaps I may be favoured with a little more information that will throw light upon it.* [32]

No response to the inquiry is recorded.

After his resignation, Stephenson was offered the circuit of Ilkley in Yorkshire. This was perhaps a way of allowing Gregory to do the job in his own way without the shadow of his great predecessor looming over him. For Stephenson, it was doubly blessed: he could return to circuit work unencumbered by the demands of the Home and he would take over as warden of the Wesleyan Deaconesses College in Ilkley, the construction of which he would oversee. Here were trained women recruited by the Church for house-to-house visitations, Bible classes, distributing tracts, nursing and social work. Such work was particularly close to his heart, for the order of deaconesses had grown very largely from the Sisterhood. The Conference did not demand that he move three years later.

In 1907 Stephenson retired from the work and returned to live in London, taking a house in Finchley. It was, at the beginning, an active retirement—he had hardly got to Finchley before he was travelling back to Leeds to attend a deaconess committee and spend the night at the college.

The 'National' Children's Home

A year later the Children's Home and Orphanage gained the prefix 'National', an indication of how far it had come from the renovated stable which the young Stephenson and his two friends had taken over. The Conference, though, recognizing the strength of feeling there was from many when his name ceased to be associated with it, decided that the words 'Founded by Dr Stephenson' should be added to the title. If there was ever disagreement between Gregory and his predecessor it was about this. Stephenson had taken no personal part in the arguments but 'it was generally supposed that the personal relations between himself and Dr Gregory... were very seriously strained by this incident.'[33] However deeply this rift was felt, the fact is that not long afterward, Stephenson, 'in grave [but unspecified] personal troubles... turned to Dr Gregory at once as a trusted friend of whose sympathy and help he was sure, and he met with a response from the latter which was as full and frank and tender as Dr Stephenson evidently felt it would be'.[34]

Gregory's health proved even less reliable than Stephenson's. Their last illnesses came upon them at the same time, and although the older man was expected to die first, it was Gregory who died on 21 June, 1912 and Stephenson who died three weeks later on 14 July. Stephenson's last illness was painful and disabling, and he had been unable to leave his home. He was nursed by Ella and also by Florence, a young woman who, as a seven-year-old orphan, had come into the Home's care. She had moved to Ilkley with the Stephensons and he had found her a good position there. But when they returned to London, she decided that she wanted to come back with them. She trained as a nurse at one of the big London teaching hospitals and came out of her training as Stephenson's last illness began. She was with him, holding his hand, when he died.

5 | Growing: the development of child care

After Stephenson's retirement in May 1900, the work of the Home continued to expand under Arthur Gregory's direction. When he became principal in 1900 there were 1,150 children in the Home's care, supported on an income of £25,285.[1] In 1911, the year before he died, the numbers had grown to 2,201, while income had almost doubled to £54,715. And there was 'one penny of debt'.[2]

By then Bonner Road had 300 children living in several properties. To the earlier chapel and school, a home for children with epilepsy and a hospital had been added. Advance elsewhere had been rapid. In 1903 Chipping Norton, Oxfordshire, was opened for children with a physical disability. In the same year Frodsham, Cheshire, was acquired. To begin the work needed to turn the hundred acres of open land with a farm and two houses into a home, three boys were transferred from Edgworth to start farming there. An aerial view of Frodsham, taken in later years, shows an imposing property set about a great circular lawn, with trees and bushes studded about. The children lived (as at Princess Alice Orphanage and other large establishments) in smaller, family-sized houses. And although, as again with Princess Alice, there was an air and a reality of self-sufficiency, the children at Frodsham went to ordinary schools in the local area and were encouraged to keep in contact with their relatives.[3]

In 1907 Bramhope in Yorkshire for boys was opened, and Leigh-on-Sea, Essex, for thirty-five girls, a year later. In 1909 Laleham Grange at Oxted, Surrey, opened. The sanatorium at Harpenden, Hertfordshire (1910), was a response to a widespread health problem—tuberculosis. One claim is that twenty-eight of every hundred of the Home's children suffered from it.[4] The Home was not the first agency to open a sanatorium but Harpenden was regarded as pioneering in its regime of continuous treatment and residential training. 'I venture to predict,' said Sir Thomas Barlow, president of the Royal College of Physicians, after a visit, 'that from this sanatorium and its work will arise in years to come enlightened effort for sick children in general who will have their lives made more wholesome, more healthy and more blessed than anything we can now provide.'[5] The year after Gregory died the Cardiff branch opened to serve south Wales.

Gregory's death in June 1912 was untimely, but never in his twelve years as principal had he stood in the shade of Stephenson. It was no empty boast that he could claim:

> ... there is no child-serving institution which covers so wide an area as ours... nor one whose care for the children is so little hampered by rules and regulations.[6]

And this 'wide area' included Canada.

That he achieved so much despite personal odds was commemorated in the somewhat florid tribute paid to him by the Rev. J. Watts-Ditchfield, vicar of Bethnal Green, in London, who referred to him as an

> heroic figure because his physical weakness, his pain and sickness were such as to cause 99 men out of a hundred to abandon so great a task, but he, with the heroism begotten of the Spirit of Christ, stuck to his work even to the last.[7]

Gregory's successor was not a young man. William Hodson Smith was fifty-seven and chairman of the Cornwall Wesleyan District. He was someone of great dramatic gifts, used in his preaching, a striking personality, and, as one who had led the equivalent of an Anglican diocese, possessed of leadership qualities. The comment that 'the homes are safe and secure for another 60 years'[8] may have seemed somewhat exaggerated in welcoming a man in late middle age, but, in fact, Hodson Smith was to lead the Home for twenty years.

The First World War, which broke out only two years after Hodson Smith had taken over, had its effects on the Home. The immediate consequence was that Canadian emigration came to a halt. But, on the home front, while contraction might have been expected, there was expansion from Newquay (to which Hodson Smith was eventually to retire) to Newcastle. The Cardiff branch would not have been alone among branches in recording, in literally the first days of the conflict: 'The hall was used for Red Cross nursing teachers.' Two months later it stated: 'A family of Belgium refugees received. They will use the lodgers' accommodation of No. 85,'[9] which was one of the two houses which made up the home. Twenty-six former boys from the Home died in the war and the Thanksgiving Appeal, launched to mark the Armistice, raised £130,000. In 1918, when arms had been laid down, ninety-seven Serbian refugees were received by the Faversham branch in Kent.

Hodson Smith's years were also ones of expansion. From 1909, three years before he took over, to 1929, four years before he put his office aside, the number of branches doubled, and the number of children residing in the homes went up by 75 per cent. In each one of these decades as many children were received as had been in the Home's first forty years. That the pattern of children's needs was changing can be seen from the fact that in the first thirty years 60 to 80 per cent of the children coming to the Home had lost one or both parents; in 1929 the number had fallen to 41 per cent.[10] For example, in the year 1923–1924, 633 children came into care. Two hundred and thirty five had lost one or both parents; ninety-eight had been deserted; one hundred and two had 'immoral or criminal parents' and had been taken from their care by the courts. Two hundred and nineteen of the children had parents who had separated, and twenty were disabled in some way.[11]

Homes, too, changed their roles to meet new needs: Ebley House, Gloucestershire, for example, was opened in 1920 for senior girls but became a residential nursery and also a training centre where girls were prepared for nursery nurse examinations. One Home project which was to serve several purposes in later years was Headlands School, Penarth, opened in 1918 as the J. H. Gibbs Home in memory of a soldier who had died in the war. In 1936 it became, uniquely, a nautical school, preparing boys for the Royal and Merchant Navies. It was later to serve as an approved school, a community home, and a special school for children with severe social, emotional and education difficulties.[12]

The headquarters of the Home had moved from Bonner Road in the summer of 1913 to City Road, near Wesley's House and Chapel. In 1925 City Road was vacated in favour of a large, handsome private house in Highbury, a pleasant suburb in north London. Two years later the Young Leaguers Union Hospital (later called a nursery) was built in the extensive grounds. (The YLU was a fund-raising organization which Stephenson had set up in 1899 to help young people help the young.)

Education of young offenders

Just as the Home had expanded and moved with the times, so had the legislative and other social forces which partly helped to shape its activities. The Children Act of 1908 had introduced more liberal treatment for young offenders, as well as taking them out of the adult judicial system with the creation of juvenile courts. But the education of delinquent children had been left behind by the development of mainstream education. Universal state education had been introduced in 1870 and became free in 1891. Central and local government were responsible for the education of children who had not come into conflict with the law, while education for young offenders fell largely to voluntary agencies, despite the increased involvement of the Home Office and the continuing need for reformatories to be 'certificated'. Up to the end of the First War, young offenders were being offered 'plain, elementary education, liberally laced with hard manual work, geared towards the status in life such children were likely to occupy in the years ahead.'[13] John Hurt has written:

> ... teaching methods were a generation behind the best
> contemporary practice. Often there was only one classroom in
> which all groups of children were taught together.[14]

But in less than a decade after the end of the war, the situation was to be transformed. In 1913 there had been a departmental committee report, the implementation of which had been delayed by the war. With the war's end the changes were dramatic: there was much greater involvement by local authorities; inspection of schools and educational establishments for young offenders by both the Home Office and the Board of Education; the closure of forty reform schools; and a dramatic fall in admissions in 1922 from 6,602 to 1,831. The result was a streamlined and efficient service, so that by the end of the 1920s

> ... the schools were better than at any other time in their history.
> They welcomed the fall in admissions as a healthy sign but
> recognised the need for such institutions for certain kinds of
> children.[15]

But these changes for juvenile offenders were not alone sufficient to reshape the service. The Children and Young Persons Act 1933 created remand homes, and welded together reformatories and industrial schools into approved schools (at Penarth and Congleton the Home provided two of the first). The approved school system was to last another thirty-six years, but the effects of its creation were the continued segregation of delinquent children in the absence of community-based alternatives, and the stigma of criminality, without regard for the social and emotional problems and other factors which often occasioned wrong-doing in the first place.

State versus voluntary sector

In the 1920s, too, came an early intimation of how the Home saw itself in the wider context of the relationships between the state and voluntary sectors. In 1921 M.A. Spielman, a former inspector with the Home Office, initiated a public discussion by claiming that 'the principle of voluntary management [of services] . . . is being seriously assailed.'[16] The principle, he went on, consisted of 'voluntary management in the hands of men and women to whom work is of a very special value and interest, who give time and labour, who bring devotion, love, self-sacrifice and spirituality to individual needs of these institutions [he was particularly concerned with industrial schools and reformatories]'.

The state, Spielman believed, could not act *in loco parentis* and neither could local authorities or paid officials meet children's individual needs. In this view he was supported by Hodson Smith, who claimed that 'people do not and will not give up their service to the State'. State management, he further asserted, would lead to an inflexible standardization and mediocrity, reduce children to types, and destroy individuality. The state, he added, would only provide officials, not parental figures, and paid officials had neither sympathy for, nor interest in those with whom they worked. Israel Ellis, head of one of the Home's industrial schools, a service for which he was a great advocate, contributed by claiming that some people, who knew nothing about the subject, had called for the abolition of the voluntary principle.[17]

This debate was to continue for decades. But the diminution of the voluntary principle was less a threat in the voluntary child care sector, where there were never serious proposals to take over its work. Local authority provision, both for children and elderly people, grew out of the reshaping of Poor Law provision, which had been a local authority service since its inception in 1601.[18]

The arguments about whether 'paid officials' can offer compassion and care are no longer heard. Local authorities are, in fact, acting *in loco parentis* with regard to some children in their care, a right which is not assumed by a voluntary agency even when the local authority has placed a child with it. The last two decades, let alone those since the Spielman debate of 1921, have lessened the distinctions in some important ways between the voluntary sector and local authorities. The former has become much more professionalized, employing more staff with professional qualifications on salaries which call for less self-sacrifice than was previously the case. Also the large subventions received by voluntary agencies, through central and local government grants, contracts and fees, means that voluntary giving is no longer the only source of income.

New adoption laws

It was in the second decade of the century also that the UK ceased to be different from the rest of Europe with the introduction, in 1926, of legal adoption—the irrevocable transfer of parental rights from birth parents to adoptive parents could now be made by court order (see chapter 4). A concern for a change in the law had come about partly through the meeting, in 1920, of the first Conference of Associated Societies for the Care and Maintenance of Infants, which had discussed the problems, then unfolding in the wake of the war, of finding satisfactory homes for unwanted children.

Another argument in favour of a change in the law was that a mother whose adoption application was rejected might fall into the hands of the unscrupulous with intentions other than the child's welfare—the procuring of girls for prostitution. She might also suffer the insecurity of having to take back her child at any time in the absence of an adoption recognized in law.

But despite these compelling reasons and the gradual weakening of a dogmatic opposition to breaking parental ties, it took two government committees, three resulting reports and six bills before Parliament between 1922 and 1924 before the Act reached the statute book. Even this did not give full rights to adoptive parents, conferring on them what the Tomlin Committee's reports in 1924 referred to as the status of 'special guardians'. The change in the law, however, still did not stop children being advertised as 'available for adoption'. It was not until 1939 that the Adoption of Children (Regulation) Act registered adoption societies like the Home, regulated their conduct, and gave local authorities supervision of children under the age of nine placed through a third party in what was, in effect, an adoption.[19]

The Home had been one of the bodies campaigning for this and many of the adoption orders made in that year 'legalized' the informal arrangements which had already existed. How many *de facto* adoptions or permanent foster placements—in effect, adoptions—were carried out by the Home before 1926 is not known with any accuracy.[20] From 1926 to 1930 there were nearly 500 adoptions; in the following five years (1931–1935) the number fell to 200, and remained that from 1936 to 1940.[21]

The Home became one of the first approved adoption agencies (local authorities were not allowed to place children for adoption until 1958). Although it placed similar numbers of boys and girls overall, significantly more girls than boys were adopted before the Second World War. In 1936 the Home's magazine *Children* stated: 'Baby boys often have to wait for a long time for a home, but the demand for baby girls far exceeds supply'[22], perhaps reflecting a belief that girls were easier to manage or more useful about the home than boys. Given the work which the Home was to do fifty years later to place older children and young people for adoption, it is interesting to note that the article went on to state:

> *Experience shows that the ideal adoption is when the baby is received in infancy, as the natural link is then more formed, but the Home arranges adoption for children up to four or five years of age, and* very occasionally for those slightly older [my emphasis].

Even in those early years, there was practice which would be considered good today. Adoptive parents were encouraged to remain in touch with the Home, to send regular reports and photographs of the children. Their letters often revealed a deep sympathy and concern for the birth parents. Children were encouraged to say a prayer for birth parents on the child's birthday. The Home was also one of the first agencies to pay adoption allowances to enable less well off families to maintain adopted children. This was necessary as at the time adopted children did not share the legal status of children born within marriage. In those days, too, the idea of matching children and parents was to be found: 'Care is taken to "match" the child to the home as far as possible, taking into account all that is known of the child and his parentage.'

One example links the early days of the new adoption law with the more recently acquired ability of those who have been adopted to trace their birth parents. In 1927 Miriam was in her mid-30s. She came from a poor family, was poorly educated and in domestic service in London with an elderly Methodist couple. She embarked on an affair with a man who, she found, when she became pregnant, was married. He abandoned her and she did not see him again. She feared turning to her family, and the elderly couple with whom she lived advised her to seek the Home's help under the new legislation as they could not have a baby in their home. She gave birth to David in Fulham and he was immediately placed with a foster mother.

After six weeks, Miriam took David to the Home's nursery at Highbury and handed him over with layette, birth certificate and rattle. Miriam never saw him again. He was adopted by a professional couple in Birmingham, who were given full written details of his birth parents and the reasons for his being placed for adoption. The adopters were encouraged to be honest with him about his adoption and they kept in touch with the Home, writing every birthday with news of his progress, often expressing concern for his mother. Some years later she contacted the Home and was assured that he was happy and healthy. In 1987 David was encouraged by his grandchildren to ask NCH for access to his records and after a search he discovered that his mother had died in an air raid in 1940.[23]

The Home, like the other child care societies, continued to expand, but its emphasis did not change. Its primary task and interest remained the provision of residential care. One of the great social changes which touched upon its own ethic was a greater secularization seen in the years following the First World War. Some of the old moralistic ways of regarding behaviour were not carried over into a society which tended to be more generally liberal and tolerant in its view of personal morality. The Home no longer spoke in the evangelistic language heard in Stephenson's day, or even under the reign of Gregory, though the Christian ethic remained its guiding principle. In a different age, too, the charismatic leadership of the early pioneers was out of fashion. Barnardo, the most charismatic leader of all, had died in 1905, Waugh of the NSPCC in 1908, Stephenson in 1912, and although Rudolf lived until 1933 he had given up the secretaryship of the Waifs and Strays in 1919.[24]

Training in child care

There was, however, one area of practice where the Home was innovatory, not only so far as the voluntary sector was concerned but within statutory services, too. This was with regard to staff training. In the very early days, Stephenson had understood that those who worked with children required not only certain qualities, but also skills which could be be acquired. As early as 1873 training had been seen by Stephenson as a safeguard against 'pious blundering'.[25] But with his going the impetus for training, basic as it may seem by modern standards, had diminished. Workers (mainly women) were trained on the job. Just as the early impulse had come from Stephenson, so it was with John H. Litten, Hodson Smith's successsor.

Litten had joined the Home's staff in 1916. Within seven months of taking over as principal in 1933 he had presented a seven-year financial and development plan to the Home's general committee. It included matters like changes in the use and organization of the branches, and staff training was prominent on the agenda. He instituted a library at Highbury and recreational facilities. He began a system of tutors and started correspondence courses, with subjects which included child study, Christian teaching, Bible study, English literature, principles of social work, and housewifery. A certificate was awarded to those who came through successfully. Litten took over a house near Highbury for students, with individual study-bedrooms.

On 18 September 1935 Stephenson Hall was opened at the back of the headquarters at a cost of £14,324. It was a purpose-built training centre. Subjects studied seem somewhat wider than the vocationally-based ones of later decades and were not greatly different from what was available on the correspondence course. They included 'Flowers in literature' and 'The development of the English novel', and essays were required on such subjects as 'The evolution of liberty', and 'The meaning of the Cross to children'. But 'The principles of social work' were studied along with 'The advantages and disadvantages of a systematic provision by the state for the relief of distress'. Training was not only of the preliminary, basic kind; refresher courses for staff who had already been through the training mill were begun. At the other end of the age spectrum, there was the Child Care Cadet Scheme for sixteen- to eighteen-year-olds to encourage an interest in working with children as a career. This scheme ran until 1968 when it was superseded by the introduction, in colleges of further education, of similar preparatory courses.

The college was the first child care training college in the country; Cecil Walpole, one time general secretary of the Home, claimed it was the first in the world.[26] In instituting specific training for residential child care workers—and Barnardo's and the Josephine Butler Memorial College were also pioneers— Litten was ahead of his time. Elsewhere, it was too often considered that 'the right personality' or training in other fields, like nursing or teaching or even the armed forces, were sufficient. In 1946 the Princess Alice College, Birmingham, was established by Audrey Wilson (later O'Dell), for the training of Sisters. Students came not only from the UK, but also from as far away as the Caribbean, Greece, South Africa, Denmark, Germany, the USA and Australia. Three years later the college and Stephenson Hall were recognized by the Home Office and staff could qualify for the Home Office's Certificate in Residential Child Care. By 1969 90 per cent of housemothers held the certificate,[27] a figure which far outweighed the numbers of residential workers in the statutory sector holding a child care qualification.

In the 1950s, the Central Training in Child Care (later the Central Council for Education and Training in Social Work), of which Litten had been appointed a member when it came into being in 1947, sponsored fourteen-month courses, including those run by the Home. These gave domestic and practical training, coupled with a study of normal growth, and the development and health of children, but there was little stress on the particular needs and background of children suffering the stress and trauma of separation or deprivation.[28] In 1947, the Council had said that a housemother should be

> ... *a person who is competent to take charge of a 'family group' of twelve to fifteen children of mixed ages and sexes, either in a small scattered Home or in a larger Home where such a group would form a 'family' within the total group. The basic idea is that staff of this type should be so trained that in addition to having domestic and other skills they should be able to meet the needs of the child as an individual in a satisfying personal relationship.*[29]

Much had been done to integrate the work of Stephenson Hall and Princess Alice College, but in 1960 the distinctions between the work of Sisters and other professional staff were so narrow that the college was closed and the two were integrated.

The training of the Sisters, while increasingly emphasizing the professional residential child care element, also had aspects peculiar to their calling. There were 350 serving Sisters in the 1930s and their studies included the Old and New Testaments, ethics, law, psychology, child guidance, and probation work. They also sat for qualifications offered by the Froebel Institute and those for nursery nurses. Part of the course was to spend between six months and two years (according to age and experience) living in one of the branches. Candidates for the Order of Sisters aged 20 and over received £30 a year, while younger ones had £25. When they had been trained they became probationer Sisters, at first for two years and later for one, before being admitted to the order. War-time austerity saw probationary Sisters being asked to contribute £6 and fifty clothing coupons to the cost of their uniforms, but they were allowed 34 days annual holiday and a day off a week.[30]

Litten's time saw other changes: babies were housed in residential nurseries, a facility to meet their special needs not best met in a family group home; under-fives went to nursery schools; while the number of children living in family group homes decreased. When work began with children who were emotionally disturbed or maladjusted, as the work of the Home widened to take in other than separated children, mental health became a component in training, and eventually qualified psychiatrists came to be used as consultants. The change, too, in the kinds of children whom the Home was increasingly helping caused the word 'orphanage' to be dropped from its title.[31] When in 1932 the various branches of Methodism were united, the Primitive Methodist Children's Homes of Alfresford, Kent, and Harrogate, Yorkshire, were incorporated within the Home's branches.

The rights of the child

One intimation of the shape of child care to come was given in 1935 by Dr T. N. Kelynack, medical secretary of the Home from 1910 to 1941, when he spoke of 'the rights of the child', a phrase redolent with preoccupations in child care fifty years later. What he said did, in some respects, also prefigure the thinking behind the Beveridge report, which was not to appear until 1942, and that of the post-war UN Declaration of Human Rights. What were these rights, he asked, and replied that they included

> ... the right to be born in love and honour ... in an environment which will provide for normal development ... a right to love, protection, care which will provide health; prevent disease; provide food, shelter, clothing, and other essentials of home growth ... the right to the affection of parents and their safeguarding by the state ... the right to shielding and direction by the Church ... the right to recreation, companionship with room for self-development ... the right to liberty and justice ... and to be safeguarded from neglect, abuse, cruelty, exploitation and every form of injustice ... the right to be treated with the regard due to a child of God.[32]

But before these ambitious post-war aims, nationally and internationally, could be realized, or at least attempted, the country was to experience the dislocation and devastation which came with the Second World War. But even before its outbreak, events in Germany were already being felt by the Home.

6 | 'I like my home because it is my home': children as refugees

At dusk each evening Hermann's father would put on his working boots and go out for a walk in the back streets of Vienna. His family thought that he wanted to take exercise but were puzzled that he never wanted them to accompany him. One night Hermann, the youngest of the three brothers, followed him and came face to face with him in Quay Street, a dimly-lit and deserted street of derelict warehouses that ran parallel with the Danube.

'What are you doing here alone?' asked the father.

'Oh nothing,' replied the son. 'Just wanted to see if the Danube Meadow was under flood.'

The elder Kauders could make no such casual excuse. His son could see that he was carrying pieces of brick embedded in concrete held in a string cradle, the ends of which were wrapped about his wrist.

Each night, the father told the son, he picked up the biggest pieces and walked up and down, practising carrying the load. He did it after dark so that no one would see him; if they did, he said, they might think him crazy. But, he explained, he wasn't. Jewish tram conductors or Jews like himself who had converted to Christianity, had been dismissed. The Nazis, he said, would come for the Jews, put them to heavy work for which he now, nightly, prepared himself. Some were already dead. No one had yet come for him because, he said, Hermann's mother was Aryan.

'Don't cry,' said the father. 'You see I want to be ready when they come. I want to be ready for hard work. That's why I am carrying the bricks. I take them in my hands and roll them and pass them from one hand to the other. The skin on my fingers is getting really tough.'

But Hermann did cry. Fifty years later he said that he could still do so.[1]

The Kauders were among 185,000 Jews who lived in Austria. In Vienna alone there were 120,000 of them. When the *Anschluss*—the annexation of Austria by Germany—took place on 12 March 1938, people were on the street where the Kauders had their flat, screaming 'Heil Hitler', giving the Nazi salute and running the swastika from their windows. A left-wing neighbour asked Mrs Kauders if she would unveil a flag. She said: 'No.' The three brothers went into the street to look for hopeful signs of empty windows but there were few. A neighbour from a floor above, having donned his swastika armband, said that he would send his wife down with flags for the Kauders. And the wife came, greatly excited, not having known that her husband was a party member.

When the schools reopened, Hermann waited for his friend Herbert Bren, a Protestant. Like him, his school friend had had to leave the classroom during the Catholic Religion Hour under the regime of Karl von Schuschnigg, the Austrian Chancellor who had effectively been unseated by the Nazis. They were left to their own devices, while the Jewish students were shepherded to another room by a rabbi. Hermann shared his coconut, Herbert shared his sweets. They saw the crowds in the streets, and Hitler riding in an open car. Bren said: 'Heil Hitler,' and grinned. Hermann self-consciously said: 'Hello,' and grinned back. Hermann said casually: 'Y'know I'm not, I'm not pure Aryan.' Herbert stopped speaking, picked up his story again as if he had not heard and when they reached a street market he brought two fig clusters and gave one to Hermann.

Their friendship, after Hermann's confession of racial 'impurity', was sealed. But could he always be so lucky? Martha, a neighbour, turned away from the family on the staircase. The five Jewish boys in the class were singled out but at least they were together. Mrs Kauders was asked by neighbours, quite casually, after the usual greeting of 'Good morning', whether she expected her husband to be shipped to Dachau. The family were made to leave their municipal flat. Mrs Kauders went from one refugee organization to another; to the evangelical church, where the children had been baptized, to receive food from the Harvest Festival; to the Bible study classes at the Swedish mission which might ease the way for carriage to Sweden.

Hermann's older brother Rudi was the first to go, to work on a farm in Lancashire in England. Soon it was Hermann's turn for the long journey by train: along the banks of the Rhine and eventually to Holland and the boat train to Harwich; then to be given white bread sandwiches for the train to Liverpool Street Station.

In the autumn of 1939, there were already other boys at Riversmead, the Home's school near Clitheroe. As the new arrivals came to the end of their journey, they might have stood by the window and looked out as the train passed under the rising beauty of Pendle Hill, which looked down on the house, and have caught the white smoke from the school's chimney.

Riversmead had become a centre for the boys after the Rev. Henry Carter, chairman of the executive committee of the Christian Council for Refugees from Germany and Central Europe, had approached the Rev. John Litten, principal of the Home. He had seen it, recently vacated and easy to adapt, as an ideal home for boys aged eleven to twelve. To bring the boys over, Henry Carter made use of the Refugee Children's Movement, an interdenominational body, based in London, which was able to undertake travel arrangements.[2]

The first party of boys had arrived from Vienna in June 1939, less than a year after Carter, who was also secretary of the social welfare committee of the Methodist Church, had been exercised about the possible fate of 'non-Aryan Christians' in Germany. With the help of George Bell, Bishop of Chichester, who was later to be a link with anti-Nazi conspirators like the theologian Dietrich Bonhoeffer, he had formed the Christian Council for Refugees from Germany and Central Europe. He became its chairman, while the Rev. Bill Simpson, a young Methodist minister working in an area of North London with a growing population of Jews, many of whom were refugees, became secretary to the council. The council was formed at a meeting in Westminster Abbey, in October 1938. Its aim, according to its annual report, was to stimulate the interest of the church in the plight of non-Aryan Christians and to raise funds for their relief.

A month before the inaugural meeting that plight had become even more acute. At the specific request of Hitler, the Nuremburg Laws had been promulgated. They forbade marriage between Jew and Gentile, as well as sexual relations in general between them, and Jews were made 'subjects' of the state, rather than having citizenship rights. Over the following few years, through supplementary enactments, Jews would be outlawed entirely, subject finally only to the decisions of the secret police, without recourse to the courts or legal protection. In many a town their situation was such that they could not obtain food, parents could not procure milk for young children, and chemists would not supply them with medicines.[3]

There had been much intermarriage in the late nineteenth century and early twentieth century, and the rates of conversion and the numbers of 'non-Aryan Christians' are almost impossible to estimate.[4] According to Reich Citizenship Law, there were two categories of *Mischlinge*, the 'mixed' offspring of Aryans and

Jews: those of the 'first degree' and those of the 'second degree'. A Jew was anyone with at least three full Jewish grandparents. Also legally defined as a Jew was someone with two full Jewish grandparents who belonged to the Jewish community when the law was passed on 15 September 1935; or who joined later; or who was married to a Jew or was the child of a marriage contracted with a Jew after 15 September 1935; or who was born out of wedlock after 31 July 1936, the offspring of extra-marital relations with a Jew. Anyone who was one eighth Jewish—that is with one Jewish great grandparent or great-great grandparent— would be considered of German blood (that is, not Jewish). A 'Mischling, first degree' was defined as a person with two Jewish grandparents, who did not otherwise fit into the categories defined as Jews (that is, was not a member of the Jewish community, was not married to a Jew, and so on). Someone with only one Jewish grandparent was a 'Mischling, second degree'.[5]

Meanwhile, the British government had tightened its laws on immigration and had laid down that those entering the UK needed some kind of guarantee from a person or organization before settlement could be allowed. Jewish emigration, largely to the UK, the USA and Palestine, had begun at the very beginning of the Nazis' accession to power. In 1933, 37,000 Jews left Germany, the highest annual figure in all the years to come. From Hitler's election as Chancellor in 1933 until November 1938, 150,000 Jews—or 30 per cent of the Jewish population of the country—left. After *Kristallnacht*, the night of 9 to 10 November 1938, when Jewish property was attacked, synagogues burned, 30,000 Jewish men rounded up and sent to concentration camps and 100 Jews murdered, another 150,000 left (those in the camps had to buy their freedom by emigrating upon release).

Hans Wolff, a former pupil at the Home's Riversmead school, was eleven when he left Germany. His father was not a devout Jew, only an occasional attender at the synagogue. He had been an active social democrat. Though there was news of this or that person being arrested, Hans and his brother did not suffer much at school and their father nurtured a faith that the German people would overthrow the Nazis. But, Hans wrote in 1985,

> *The turning point came on ... Kristallnacht, when my father, in common with other Jewish males, was arrested at about 5 in the morning and taken to Buchenwald concentration camp. No one knew the whereabouts of the Jewish men who had been rounded up for some time but gradually, after three weeks, the first victims of this dreadful persecution began to drift back with whispers of the horrors and deprivations they had suffered. They had to sign documents as to their*

good treatment before release—with warnings of dire consequences of
loose talk. Some did not return. From our town the young rabbi and
his father were murdered. My father returned shortly before
Christmas, and it was after this experience that my parents, with little
chance of emigrating as a family unit, decided, on hearing of the
Pfarrer Grueber organisation [a body which assisted the emigration of
Jewish children], to enrol me, then aged eleven and my brother aged
seven, to get us to safety out of Nazi Germany and then decide on
action for their own preservation.

In Austria thousand of Jews were fleeing. Hermann Kauders and his brother
were two of 126,000 Austrian Jews who had left their country by the end of
1939—120,000 of them before the outbreak of war.

Riversmead

The Kauders' home had been one of sixty-five addresses in Austria and
Germany to have received a letter in June 1939 advertising Riversmead: it
would have seventy pupils, said the letter, four teachers, five Sisters and a
cook. 'Letters may only be sent on Sundays,' it stipulated, adding that parcels
and sweets were distributed on Wednesday and Sunday. 'Riversmead is a
modern school, that is to say, discipline is a matter of form and behaviour, not
an end in itself. Punishments are kept to a minimum—chiefly there is a
morning detention and Wednesday and Sunday detention up to an hour.'
(This proved to be not wholly correct at the beginning in at least one instance:
one German teacher was asked to leave eventually as his methods did not
accord with those of the school. A punishment which he practised was to lock
erring pupils in a completely dark coal cellar.) The letter ended: 'Our
principles are: honesty, attention to duty, independence and readiness to help.'

But there was much to be done in Riversmead. Henry Carter's Christian
Council gave the Home £9,000. An initial £1,643 paid for building repairs,
furnishings and a new sanitary block. Three house rooms, dormitories,
schoolrooms, a large dining room, a gymnasium, staff bedrooms, a sitting
room, and a teachers' common room were redecorated, along with washing
and toilet facilities. The playing fields and the tarmacked areas were also
attended to. Three bilingual Sisters from the Home were transferred to the
school and there were some German teachers.

The first contingent numbered thirty-five boys. They wore Tyrolean dress
and none of them spoke English. Their unexpectedly wide age-range—they

were aged nine to sixteen—meant that school plans had to be remodelled and the original plans for dividing into houses had to be rethought. When the first German boys arrived there was an initial tension: refugees or not, these were from the land of the aggressor. But when an Austrian boy was assigned to befriend and help each German boy, the tension was ended.

The relationships, though, were not without difficulties and some of the boys were teased about their Jewish-looking appearance. Hermann Kauders later said that the age barriers were formidable obstacles to overcome and that lasting friendships between younger and older boys never took root. On the other hand, Karl Arie, half a century later, wrote that his oldest friends were those he had met at Riversmead: they were, he said, 'more like a family'.

Horace Cahill, a local businessman, who chaired a local support committee for the project, interviewed in *The Riversmead Record*, spoke of the condition of many of the boys upon arrival:

> *Many of the boys bore unmistakable signs of their experiences in Nazi Germany, and for some time after their arrival their health was a matter of great concern to the Sisters of Riversmead. The younger boys, in particular, suffered from great nervous strain and were subject to horrible nightmares, presumably as a result of severe shock or the memory of some incidents. When they arrived only a few of the boys could speak any English, but now (four months later) all of them are able to converse freely and some of the older boys are attending the Clitheroe technical evening school.*

Riversmead's day was little different from that of many other English boarding schools. It began at 6.30, with prayers at 7.45, followed by breakfast a quarter of an hour later. After that a clinic was available for anyone feeling unwell and the school bell rang at 8.50. Physical training, music and crafts had their place on the curriculum. Dinner was at 6 p.m. Evening activities included chess and other games, or talking. There was a good library and, on summer evenings, some boys gardened. The boys learned to play cricket and also played football against other local schools. One former pupil, Hans Wolff, wrote:

> *Riversmead was very much a closed community, and apart from tradesmen delivering groceries etc—Farmer Jackson, who was a neighbour and dealt with the boilers—and visits to chapel on Sundays we did not come into contact with too many people. A Scout group was formed and through this we met Scoutmasters and*

*boys from the locality but these were occasional contacts and not
the basis for lasting acquaintance or friendships for most of us.*

There were three forms (later extended to five) into which the boys were slotted on the basis of intelligence and achievement. Some would transfer eventually to other of the Home's branches where they would learn farming; others gained scholarships to Queen's College, Taunton; some took a course leading to the School Certificate; while others attended technical classes in the evening at Clitheroe Technical School until it was convenient to enter a technical day school.

When war broke out on 3 September 1939, there were sixty-five boys on the roll. How they appreciated their new surroundings, despite living in a strange country, their uncertainties and fears about parents and other relatives whom they had left behind, can be gauged in the essays they wrote in the early weeks on 'Why I love Riversmead'. There was the expected enjoyment in excursions, the garden, the beauty of the countryside and the nearness to the sea and the mountains, the handsome house, woods and meadows, and games. Hans, aged twelve, wrote:

> *I like Riversmead very well because we can have games here. In
> Germany we were excluded from games of all kinds for the reason
> we were considered Jews. Here in Riversmead we start a new life for
> it does not matter to anyone whether we are Jews or Christians.*

But for all the evocation of the countryside, the delight in games and so on, there was the simple thought, expressed by one boy: 'I like my home because it is my home.'

Most of the boys ceased to receive letters when the war came. But each Sunday they were still encouraged to write. On the day that war was declared, one boy wrote:

> *Dear mother, I still received your letter which I cannot answer. I am
> very glad to acknowledge the receipt of Aunt Clara's parcel. Dear
> mother, are you well? I wonder how things are there? We are well
> looked after and play games as before. You know how I like
> football, it keeps you from thinking too much, but at night, when I
> have gone to bed, I have to think of you. I know you will be
> worrying. And then I long to be with you. If only I would know how
> you and the family are.*

Another wrote:

> *Today war has broken out between England and Germany. No*
> *longer are we allowed to leave our premises except with a Sister or*
> *master. Many boys have cried. With the last post I received a parcel*
> *from Aunt Anna.*

During the summer Heinz Schulmeister, another pupil, received letters from home detailing his parents' desperate efforts to leave Germany; their anxiety about their situation was intertwined with their anxiety about their son: should they send him a blanket? He had to remember that *Apparat* was spelled with two 'p's. Through a contact in Holland he continued to correspond with them after September 1939. His twentieth letter arrived in Berlin just before Christmas, and he received this reply from his father: 'You can't imagine what difference news from you made to our Christmas. Mother was radiant with joy...'

As the boys reached the age of sixteen they were required to attend a tribunal in Leeds, eventually to be registered as 'C' category aliens, which meant that they were subject only to the most minimal restrictions. But with the outbreak of war, some local sympathy for refugees was transformed into suspicion at natives of the enemy country. The only material result of this was that the local policeman came to confiscate cameras but, finding that he had nowhere to store them, returned them to staff for safe keeping. In 1940, with internment of German males over the age of forty, the school was bereft of its German teaching staff. Audrey O'Dell, who spoke German and was lecturing at the Home's college in London, joined the staff, with Mollie Coleman, the Home's educational psychologist.

O'Dell recounts how a religious instruction lesson brought home to her what some of the boys had suffered before coming to England. They were studying the story of the Passion :

> *One of them [the boys] was reading: 'Then they spat in his face and*
> *struck him; and some slapped him, saying ...', and immediately*
> *they all laughed. I was horrified and about to reprimand them*
> *when suddenly I knew why. They understood this in a way I could*
> *not. No one had ever spat on me or struck me in that violent,*
> *insulting way. I understood it from the outside, but they had seen it*
> *happen or maybe had been spat at or struck themselves when they*
> *were accused of being Jews. Their only defence was to laugh—the*

alternative was to break down and cry. That would have brought
more insults. To take it all to heart would have made life
impossible.

On 11 July 1942 Riversmead closed. The house was to be readapted yet again and given over to the care of babies. Smaller premises were taken for the boys who remained at 94 Preston Road, Blackburn, also called Riversmead. By Christmas of that year there were twenty boys in the Blackburn hostel, with eleven in lodgings in Clitheroe who had jobs locally. Ten lived and worked in Birmingham and five lodged in Blackburn. Five were at the home at Edgworth and five in London. Two boys had gone to the USA and nine were working in Yorkshire or Lancashire. One was in the Army and one in the Merchant Navy.

Norman Taylor, someone who had helped with the Blackburn home, wrote in 1943 of Christmas there:

> *The experience of spending Christmas Eve in the company of*
> *Austrians was a delightful and novel one to me. As, in the*
> *candlelight, we entered into a real international fellowship, we*
> *wished that the world might imitate our example and come to rely*
> *on friendships instead of battleships. Naturally, our feelings were*
> *mixed: many of us were thinking of other days and times and all of*
> *us were looking forward to the time when goodwill toward all men*
> *would be a reality.*

But, as the war drew on, the boys were drawn into the conflict more directly: eighteen of them joined the forces; some fought in Europe, others in Burma. Three fought with the Americans and one joined the Australian army. Oskar Janowitz was taken prisoner. Travelling in a cattle truck with other prisoners he grew incensed at a German guard who ignored a sick prisoner and swore at him. 'You speak good German,' the guard said. 'Where do you come from?' Had he admitted he was Viennese, he would have been shot. As it was, he said that his father had worked in Vienna, and, as a child, he had lived there. Another boy, Robert Schlesinger, was confronted at the battle of Arnhem by an old school fellow, now a German soldier, who took him prisoner. But neither he nor the soldier revealed his origins and he eventually escaped.

Gunther (or Eric, as he called himself) Selig, one of the outstanding pupils, who had a father incarcerated in a concentration camp, volunteered for service in the British Army. Before leaving he wrote in *The Riversmead Monitor*:

This is the fifth year we have been over here. All of us had some glorious experiences, made friends, and generally speaking, have received a different outlook on life. Let us hope that when this struggle is over and we go our separate ways, we may, armed with those experiences, have a hand in forming the long wished for world-wide Brotherhood of Nations. It will not be long now.

Gunther was killed in action. After the war, one of the Home's Sisters, Laura Evans, went to Germany and visited his mother. Here was to be seen what the tragedy of war and the defeat of their country had meant to one German family. The woman's husband had died in the camp, and her other son, a German conscript, had perished on the Russian front.

With the war at an end, the Riversmead community scattered. Audrey O'Dell, by now principal of the Home's training college, became a channel for news of parents and relatives. She had to tell one boy that his mother had been consumed in the death factory of Auschwitz ('that night I shall never forget'). But for another boy there was happier, even astonishing news. His father had spent the war living in the Vienna woods, with his mother taking him food and spending time with him when it was safe to do so. In leaving the house she had had to be careful not to be observed by neighbours who might have betrayed her.

After he had left Riversmead Hermann Kauders had a letter from a woman in Kidderminster saying that she had met his brother Paul in a local sugar-beet factory and that he was a prisoner of war in a camp nearby. Hermann travelled to see him and spoke to him through the camp wire. Paul had remained in Austria and had been conscripted to a forced labour unit working in Normandy. With the Allied advance, the units had disintegrated and he had found himself wandering in rural France. He joined the French Resistance but was wearing his labour unit uniform when the American army had come upon him and arrested him. He was transferred to the UK.

Hermann's other brother, Rudi, who had left Austria before him and been settled in Lancashire, had met Hermann when he was at Riversmead. Rudi was in the British Army and when he returned home on leave, the three brothers were united. They learned later that their parents, too, had survived the war.

7 | All change: the brave new post-war world

The aftermath of the First War had quickly ushered in a deep sense of disillusion, a realization by the mass of the people that Lloyd George's promise of 'homes fit for heroes to live in' was a cruelly empty one. By contrast, even during the course of the Second War there were intimations that things would not be the same again. The coalition government, with its strong Labour participation, had established a Ministry of Reconstruction, under Lord Reith, to look beyond the war. In 1944 the urgent considerations of overcoming the final obstacles to achieving victory did not prevent the passing of the Education Act, with its main theme, in the words of its architect the President of the Board of Education, R.A. Butler, to 'develop a full secondary education for all'.[1]

The general election of 1945 ushered in the great Labour majority, signifying the country's desire to throw off the pre-war world of poverty and mass unemployment, along with political complacency and inaction with which they had been faced. Although nearly 400,000 members of the armed forces, the Merchant Navy and civilian Britons had died in the war, the employed population, thanks partly to an increase in the labour force, and partly to the virtual elimination of unemployment, was three million strong. Unlike the First World War, the Second had stimulated and created new industries. As one historian has remarked:

> *The very spirit of the nation had changed. No one in 1945 wanted to go back to 1939. The majority were determined to go forward and were confident that they could do so.*[2]

The effect of the war on the National Children's Home had been practical—branches in evacuation reception areas took on responsibility for children leaving the cities threatened with, and subject to, bombing. The great movement of the child population meant that nine of its thirty branches were temporarily closed; but such were war-time needs that by 1943 there were thirty-six branches. The Home also continued to care for refugee children who had come to England from Austria and Germany in the days before the outbreak of war (see chapter 6).

The war was to recast society and the Home. John H. Litten was far-sighted enough to see this. He established a Commission on Reconstruction and founded a reconstruction fund. The latter was intended not only to make good the losses to the organization's property caused by the war but also to see that the organization's work could be taken forward in the newly emerging world. The losses to property had been few (the home at Bonner Road had moved to Harpenden in 1912, but the old buildings had been blitzed). Litten sought the advice of the Board of Education on the future development of the Home. It thought that the Home should organize its educational facilities along the lines by which secondary education would be shaped nationally by the Education Act; streaming by age, and segregation on the basis of technical, grammar and so-called secondary modern education. Litten went against the Board's advice. He wanted all-age, mixed sex facilities, with nursery education for under-fives.[3]

The Home's reconstruction report was published in 1942. Much of it was concerned with new developments. There were the immediate needs, bringing back from 'exile', as Litten wrote at the time, the Home's scattered family.[4] But while the losses to property had not been great, the Commission had offered the opportunity to look afresh at how well the organization was served by what it had. Some of the homes needed additions or rebuilding. A new property, Brackley, donated during the war, had to be brought into use. Others needed conversion to suit different needs. The need for more baby and nursery homes was seen by Litten as 'a great and insistent one'.

Litten concluded:

> *The Children's Home has always made it a primary objective to be a real home rather than merely an institution. Here are the methods proposed by the Reconstruction Commission for the preservation of its home life: wise, sympathetic, and understanding heads of various households; a spirit of ready co-operation throughout the entire*

family; a scheme of living in which each individual child has his recognised place; a sense of security; a certain degree of responsibility in the day's routine; a reasonable standard of comfort, adequate food, suitable clothing, and varied interests; and happy home memories, with a place of glad return throughout the years to follow...

More than a home, a hospital, a school and a workshop, the Children's Home is a church in the sense that it seeks to direct the feet of those setting out on life's journey into ways of Christian discipleship. This it endeavours to accomplish by the example of good men and women, by the religious training of home and school life, by public worship, and by the preparation of its older girls and boys to take their places in the membership of the churches of their upbringing, or of their choice.[5]

The Children's Charter

In 1948 the organization adopted a Children's Creed as part of its Children's Charter. This laid down some guiding, if high-sounding principles:

I believe in the unity of education for the body, the mind and the soul, and that childhood's unfolding life should be aided by a progressive scheme of instruction, example and helpfulness which seeks for the growth of personality and education, a knowledge of truth, and the power to do.

I believe that every child is more than the child of his parents, but carries with him some part of the common inheritance of the human race, and some part of its promise of future achievement. And I believe that it is the educator's privilege and responsibility to discover and liberate these potential values.

I believe that every child should have timely and suitable conditions for development up to the full level of his ability, so that the child may be placed and helped accordingly.

I believe that education is for living and not merely for making a living, that, for the discovery and fulfilment of life, all a child's faculties must be regarded as parts of a unified personality, which for its true development must find its fitting place in human relationships, in a widening service to humanity, and to the greater glory of God.[6]

To give practical effect to this, the National Children's Home said that what was required was 'a wise, sympathetic and understanding' head of the household; co-operation within the family (of the Home); and giving each child its recognized place in the scheme of living, a sense of security, a share in the day's routine, and a reasonable standard of comfort, adequate food, suitable clothing and varied interests. Religious 'training' was to be sought through the example of both men and women, the 'daily practice of homely religion', religious teaching in day and Sunday school, and a 'fitting place' for children in 'Christian worship and churchmanship'.

The Charter also gave attention to progressive methods of technical and general education and psychological assessment of aptitude and abilities. Plans were to be made for the aftercare and careers of young people. Through the Charter the organization turned its mind to children with special needs, like those who were disabled, 'long-term invalids', 'backward' children, offenders, and 'especially the maladjusted children who bear in body, mind and spirit the deep-graven marks of neglect and wrong doing'.[7]

Litten's changes in training and the life of the Home's branches had made the organization's child care policies and practice more progressive. It had shown Litten's mettle as an innovator and leader. In 1950, John Waterhouse, who had sat on the governing executive committee since 1944, joined him as his vice-principal. He was to prove an able lieutenant but in the immediate post-war years Litten was to play a part on a wider stage in work which was to reshape not only the Home and other child care agencies, but the whole structure of child care throughout the country.

The Curtis Committee

The war had evoked a greater public consciousness about children deprived of family life. Evacuating all children, including those children who lived in Poor Law institutions and in children's homes such as Barnardo's, the Home and the Waifs and Strays (now The Children's Society), had increased awareness of those children's lives. Families who had, perhaps, never known much at all about children who lived in residential care came to understand what it meant for families to be divided, and experience the pain of separation from parents, brothers and sisters. Into this growing concern fell two explosive devices which together were to shatter any lingering assumptions about children in care and the way they were cared for.

In 1944 Lady Allen of Hurtwood wrote a letter to *The Times* which voiced these emerging concerns:

> *I write of those children, who, because of their family misfortune*
> *find themselves under the guardianship of a Government*
> *Department or one of the many charitable organisations. The public*
> *are... unaware that many thousands of these children are being*
> *brought up under repressive conditions that are generations out of*
> *date and are unworthy of our traditional care for children. Many*
> *who are orphaned, destitute or neglected still live under the chilly*
> *stigma of 'charity'.*[8]

The staff, she added, were 'for the most part overworked, underpaid and untrained'. She criticized the lack of a recognized training system; the inadequate inspection and supervision. This provoked an enormous response in the newspaper's correspondence columns. Six months later she put her argument more substantially in a pamphlet, *Whose Children?*.[9] Lady Allen's propaganda pot continued to boil. In her letter she had called for a public inquiry. Whether her efforts alone would have secured one we do not know, but within days of the publication of her pamphlet, the second event occurred which was to make that call irresistible.

The inquest into the death of thirteen-year-old Dennis O'Neill, who had been beaten and starved to death by his foster father in January 1945, was widely reported in the press. He had been boarded out in a remote farmhouse in Shropshire by his local authority. The jury's verdict concluded with criticism of the local authority's lack of supervision. There was an immediate public inquiry into the O'Neill case but the government then established an official committee, chaired by Miss Myra Curtis, to investigate the care of children 'deprived of normal home life with their own parents or relatives'. It was empowered to discover what more should be done to 'ensure that these children are brought up under conditions best calculated to compensate for the lack of parental care'. John Litten was appointed a member of what came to be known as the Curtis Committee.

The committee cast its net wide: destitute children, homeless evacuees, children awaiting adoption, children thought ineducable, children with a psychiatric problem, children with a learning difficulty, physically disabled children, children orphaned in the war—all became part of its concern; 125,000 of them, it has been estimated.[10] Litten's appointment said much for the standing of the National Children's Home. In some ways it had to change but in many ways it was free from the report's strictures. For example, the committee had found 'a widespread and deplorable shortage of the right kind of staff, personally qualified and trained to provide the child with a substitute home background. The result in many homes was a lack of personal interest in and affection for the children which we found shocking. The child in these Homes was not recognized as an individual with his rights and possessions, his own life to live and his own contribution to offer.'[11] It had been Stephenson's intention from the very beginning for the Home to create some approximation of the family home for the children in his care, and as far back as 1873 the Home had seen training as a safeguard against 'pious blundering'.[12] Nor could the Home be found guilty of Curtis' accusation that some children's homes were characterized by 'dirt and dreariness, drabness and over regimentation'.[13]

Others did not receive the committee's findings so readily. Barnardo's stated that 'the report can teach us little in regard to general recommendations for child care'. Any deficiencies Barnardo's might have had were due to the shortages of staff and equipment in war time. Barnado's believed that the threat of state interference through inspection would curtail the organization's 'freedom of action'.[14] The Home was more positive in its responses. Reorganising child care, it said, would not imperil its work; indeed, it quoted the government's acceptance of the Curtis Committee's belief that 'voluntary agencies should be free to continue their present activities in the care of children'. As if to emphasize that relations between this voluntary agency and the state were on a sound footing and that the future held only promise, it referred to the 'happy' co-operation between itself and the state—the helpfulness of the Ministry of Health inspections, its five approved schools and the Home Office inspectorate.[15]

Barnardo's, like the Home, could not be faulted with regard to training. But apart from that which it and the Home provided, training of residential staff was unknown.[16] Indeed, the National Children's Home underlined this fact by pointing to its training as examples of what Curtis envisaged—two years spent partly in study, partly in a home, to be followed by a year in a home with an arranged course of study culminating in the production of a thesis.[17]

There was an historical inevitability about Curtis that made radical change unstoppable. It favoured adoption, with fostering as the second best, for children who could not be cared for by their natural families. Residential care was the least favoured option. But where there was to be institutional care, homes should be small—eight children to a home and not more than twelve—while children should be encouraged to make friends outside the home and to keep in touch with relatives; brothers and sisters should be brought up together.

The Children Act 1948

Some of the Curtis philosophy had to wait many years, even decades, for acceptance, particularly the idea that residential care was not the preferred form of care for children. But much of what it recommended was carried out in the Children Act 1948. The immediate and most far-reaching effect of this was the creation of local authority children's departments under a children's officer.

Under the provisions of the Act, the Home became a registered adoption society and its homes, like all voluntary homes, made subject to inspection. Perhaps the most critical implication for voluntary bodies was that the Act required the children's officers to act as good parents 'to further [the child's] best interests and to afford him the opportunity for proper development of his character and abilities'. The voluntary agencies would also see that as their role, but, of most significance, such responsibility was no longer largely a charitable concern.

Bodies like the Home and Barnardo's which had a religious basis for their work, were also affected by another legislative provision which was that a child should be given 'a religious upbringing appropriate to the persuasion to which he belongs'. Thus, it would be henceforth unlawful not to recognize, say, a child's Catholic upbringing, or even an upbringing in a non-Christian faith.

One longer-term consequence of the Children Act was that standards in public care were to improve and as they did, the numbers of children in voluntary care declined. There were 33,000 children in voluntary care at the time of the Curtis Report. In 1971, when another great reorganization of social services was under way as the Seebohm reforms created social services departments, the numbers were 11,500.[18]

The Children Act's stipulation that all children in care were to be fostered unless this was 'not practicable or desirable for the time being' was, over time, to have a marked effect on patterns of child care. It was partly responsible for the eventual turning against residential care, which saw both local authorities and child care charities, like the Home, closing establishments and having a more vigorous approach to placing children, even those 'hard to place', in adoptive or foster homes.

In the Home's first hundred years it was estimated that there were 8,000 adoptions[19], with applications running in later years at 1,500 a year. In the centenary year of 1969 there were 304 adoptions.[20] In 1966–67, 3,535 children were looked after by the Home, 2,716 of them in residential care.[21]

In 1975 the organization looked after 2,346 children in residential care, 1,229 were cared for in the community, and 1,239 took advantage of its day care.[22] The next year there were 2,540 children in residential care, 1,500 in the community and 1,325 in day care.[23]

As the third largest voluntary child care agency—it was not for some while that the Home went into second place after Barnardo's—the Home had also to count its bank balance as well as the numbers of children it helped. In the centenary year (1969) the running costs of the Home were £1,772,795.[24] In 1964–65 it had reached the £1 million mark, while in 1948, the year that the Children Act was passed, it had been half that sum. In 1966–67 voluntary income was £736,560, an increase of £26,100 over the previous year.[25] (Ten years before it had stood at not quite half a million pounds.) Over the years the amount of money coming from government and local authorities grew. Local authorities paid fees to the Home for placing children in its care but also, like the government, they would fund it to carry out work, or to go into partnership with it. But voluntary income remained (and remains) important, be it the annual street corner collection, the jumble sale, the fund-raising dinner or the large donation from companies (see chapter 11). But the National Children's Home, like other voluntary agencies, was not immune to the swings of the economy. In 1973–74, for example, inflation outstripped voluntary income in real terms for the first time.[26]

There was to be, too, a reaction against the idea of 'rescue': the belief that, as if by surgical incision, children could be taken out of damaging homes and given new ones and all would be well. To people like Stephenson and the other pioneers, seeing the Dickensian poverty and cruelty about them, it was a most reasonable belief—the emigration policies were perhaps the most extreme manifestation of this. But one tenet working against 'rescue' was that many families, even the most deprived, could be worked with, could be helped, so that their children need not be given up for adoption. Such families might be helped by family centres, preventative work, short-term foster placements, or respite care. The natural place for many children was in the home into which they were born. By the same token, it came to be gradually recognized that children born with a disability, even a severe physical or mental one, ought not to go into residential care, no matter how benevolent. Many could, with enough resources offered to the family, continue to live in their own homes, and enjoy those facilities enjoyed by their non-disabled brothers and sisters.

The Home had pioneered the small family home in the great period of expansion before the First World War and in the years after it, but some of its properties were no longer small, even if their regimes were domestic rather than institutional. Some of the properties that came its way by donation did not easily make for small group living. Under Litten, moves were made to recreate small homes. But the great burden of change for much of the post-war period fell on John Waterhouse, who succeeded Litten as principal in 1950. Like his predecessor, he was to see his job as having a national dimension so that, for example, he, like Litten, served as a member of the official Central Training Council in Child Care, one of the ancestors of the present Central Council for Education and Training in Social Work.

In retirement Litten went to Australia with a party of the Home's children and three Sisters (see chapter 3). It was the last gasp of the emigration policy. Children had ceased to go to Canada and Litten hoped that the boys and girls he took with him would be good advertisements for a training programme he hoped to promote. But the thrust of policy was now moving firmly against such initiatives. Litten died in 1954.

The Children and Young Persons Act 1969

There was other legislation which helped shape the Home's direction. One of the most significant pieces was the Children and Young Persons Act 1969. The Curtis Committee had not found fault with the approved schools, but as one commentator wrote:

> ...*Their chief fault appeared to be the lack of feminine influence and a tendency to regimentation, with lack of opportunity for individual interests.*[27]

This was not the most substantial criticism levelled at the schools. They had singularly failed to deal with the problem of juvenile offending. Their approach was punitive; and they were detached from the circumstances in which the offenders had found themselves. Approved schools now seemed to mirror the adult prison: more and more offenders were being sent there with less and less effect on their subsequent behaviour. Another problem was that after the Second World War assessment centres had been founded to send offenders to whichever approved school seemed most likely to help. The intention was good, but the effect was that some youngsters were sent hundreds of miles from home.

Over the previous years much thinking had gone into looking at the perceived faults of the system and working out an alternative. As Eileen Younghusband remarks:

*Throughout the 1960s young delinquents continued to be albeit
unwittingly the most effective pressure group for changes in the
ways of dealing with them and for a family service.[28]*

The system had to its credit, she says, the Children and Young Persons Act
1963 which had sought to reduce the number of young people going into care
by giving advice, help and cash to families with problems, but without offering
additional resources to the children's departments (this was to be one of the
claims of how the 1969 Act was undermined).

The following year came the influential Labour Party report, chaired by
Lord Longford, *Crime: A Challenge to Us All*,[29] which, among other things,
anticipated the 1968 Seebohm report in supporting a family service. That year,
too, several members of the group found themselves members of the new
Labour government under Harold Wilson. One result of this was the 1965
White Paper, *The Child, the Family and the Young Offender*,[30] which favoured
abolishing juvenile courts and replacing them with family councils for those
under sixteen, as well as creating family courts.

Under the legislation, approved schools (together with detention centres,
remand homes and assessment centres) would be merged into new
community homes. The White Paper did not meet with universal approval
but its prescriptions for the future of approved schools were to bear fruit, albeit
by way of a second White Paper, in 1968, *Children in Trouble*[31]. In all this
agitation for change the National Children's Home was active. In the four years
leading up to the 1969 Act it had consulted with children's departments, other
voluntary agencies and the regional inspectorates of the Home Office to
ensure that the voluntary agencies' contribution to discussion and decision
making was effective. It proved to be so.

The 1969 Act sought to move from the idea of punishment to treatment,
and the philosophy of the new policy was summed up by the White Paper,
Children in Trouble, which foreshadowed the Act:

*Action by society to deal with children in trouble should be designed
where possible to support the child in the family, encouraging and
helping parents to fulfill their responsibilities and preserving the
client's links with his local community.[32]*

As well as community homes there was also intermediate treatment, which
meant that a juvenile court could order an offender to take part in a local
activity for a month or more. (This was not like community service orders for

adult offenders, where the work had to be of some social usefulness; it often had youngsters engaging in outdoor pursuits like hiking or camping.) The new community homes were meant to be part of a continuum of care and their control and management passed from the hands of the Home Office to the new social services departments (unified welfare departments created in 1971, which had absorbed the children's departments). And so bodies like the Home, which had run approved schools, regained 'a considerable degree of control and autonomy'.[33]

But while this was a new dawn for the liberal reformers in the voluntary agencies, the government and the social services departments, even as it broke, the gathering clouds could already be seen. The main objective of the new Act was to keep young people out of the courts and to do so by creating informal contacts between services and within the family. The arguments in Parliament centred around the old question of 'deprived or depraved', and while the 'welfare principle' won the day on the floor of the House of Commons and the Act reached the statute book, the contrary arguments never went away.

A decade later those favouring the 'depraved' view, who believed that wrongdoing had to be met with punishment, not treatment and care, had their revenge. The institution of the then Home Secretary William Whitelaw's 'short, sharp shock' regimes in detention centres, though later discredited, augured another period when policies were far removed from the intentions of the 1969 Act, which was gradually consigned to the wastepaper basket of social policy.

At the same time, liberal forces were undermining the community homes. Care in the community was gathering pace, and while those who favoured it would have no truck with the short, sharp shockers, community homes were becoming tarred by the same brush which was painting so poor a picture of residential care generally. Professional fostering—the recognition that high fees needed to be paid to foster families who would take in often very difficult youngsters, some of whom might have a background of offending—was becoming fashionable. This was pushing social services, including the voluntary sector, in new directions. Thus, in 1984 the Bonnington Report from the Social Care Association, one of the leading professional bodies, among whose members were numbered many residential care workers, could say:

> *Prime consideration is now given to supporting families in the care*
> *of their children, rather than supplanting the parents or removing*

the children into care. When an alternative is required, fostering and adoption are usually considered first.[34]

There were other changes for the Home sought to respond to. For example, because at one time one child in five taken into its care had suffered from pulmonary tuberculosis[35] Harpenden had become a sanatorium in 1916. By the mid-1950s TB was virtually a thing of the past and Harpenden was put to other uses: at one time it was an arrival point for fifty orphaned baby girls from Hong Kong. Edgworth, like some other homes, became a special school for children with educational difficulties. In the 1930s Alverstoke, Hampshire, became a 'Sunshine House' for children with rickets. After the war, when rickets was no more, the home housed refugee children from Germany and Austria. It later became a residential school for physically disabled girls. In the late 1960s such developments in health care meant the closing down of two units for diabetic children. There were two schools for what were then called educationally subnormal children; three approved schools had been opened for juvenile offenders; six branches catered specifically for babies; while there were three residential schools for physically disabled children.[36]

During Waterhouse's nineteen-year tenure, nineteen branches opened, fourteen closed and eight changed their use. Some places which closed were old and unsuitable (like the approved school at Newcastle upon Tyne); others were inconveniently situated to serve children needing help; and others—like the Netherton Nursery at Frodsham, the Ashfield Nursery, and the Barton House Nursery at Harrogate—were used for special purposes and so not easily adaptable for other uses.[37] In 1954 the first Scottish branch of the Home opened at Cathkin House, Ruthglen, but it was to be another twelve years before it was joined by a second, Archie Briggs House at Pitlochry.

One, perhaps unforeseen, secondary effect of the Children Act had been that the new children's departments created alternative, attractive careers for women—a majority of the first children's officers were women—and this, and the fact that other opportunities for women to work expanded after the war, meant that the proportion of men to women working for the Home grew. The new opportunities in social work for everyone, whatever their gender, meant that staff could no longer be relied upon to see the work as a vocation. The Sisterhood, of course, continued for many years. There were men in the ordained ministry still attracted to the Home's work—the principal was to continue to be drawn from their ranks until the present decade—but it adopted national salary scales for residential and fieldwork staff, as it had previously adopted such scales for its teaching and nursing staff. More married couples, too, came forward (perhaps this was an unexpected development), and often trained side by side.

8 | A place in the sun: NCH Action For Children's work overseas

At first sight it may seem a historical curiosity that, in 1969, as the tide of colonialism throughout the world had almost completely receded, the Home came to the Eastern Caribbean, still today the largest focus of its work overseas. At that time the Home saw itself as having a missionary role.[1] But this was less a matter of evangelization (the Caribbean has a strong Christian tradition, anyway) than a belief that it could celebrate its centenary year by offering to help a developing country meet its many needs in the welfare field. Inquiries were made in twenty-six countries about the possibility of working abroad.[2] Eventually, the Caribbean was settled on: street children, disability and child care training were strong features in the work of the Home which would dovetail with the particular needs of the region.

Initially the work began in Barbados and St Lucia and, within a short time, expanded to St Vincent, Dominica, Grenada and Belize. By the end of the Home's first decade in the area, concerns about race and culture and their implications for social work practice were expressing themselves in the UK. Equal opportunities policies, race awareness training programmes, the special needs of clients from different black and ethnic minority groups, the shortcomings of the 'colour blind' approach to the provision of services were making themselves felt. A white agency, rooted in British social work, working in a black English-speaking part of the world, could not be immune to this. The Home, starting from scratch with local staff but, initially, an imported management, responded to growing concerns about cultural sensitivity, recognizing the anomalies of its position at the same time as the need for its work, and the need to make changes in staffing and practice along the way. Today, NCH Action For Children continues its work in the Eastern Caribbean.

In the West Indies the Home's relationship with both the East Caribbean and the Jamaican enterprises (NCH came to Jamaica in 1973) was a parental one: it gave them birth. It saw its role as offering training and technical assistance, supporting community initiatives and working with a community development approach. NCH Action For Children came from a country where it is one of a number of voluntary childcare agencies—albeit the second largest—and where the authorities have an extensive role in provision. Working on small islands meant that the agency would be a very visible local presence. Small issues can be magnified for political purposes; a change of government or personnel can mean a change of direction of policy; and the speed of decision making, both negative and positive, is much quicker.

The agency came to Jamaica originally to provide residential care facilities and a twelve-month training programme for senior child care officers throughout the Caribbean. That first residential accommodation was designed to include a training centre. For six years it worked well, but was eventually discontinued because the Caribbean government and other organizations were unable to maintain the necessary level of support.

Jamaica is now a 40-bed children's home (divided into three units), where more than a third of the children are disabled. There is also a 40-bed unit for children with severe multiple disabilities, and a day school for fifty youngsters (which serves both the residential unit and the Kingston community).

In Barbados, NCH Action For Children undertakes staff training. It also works with the national Child Care Board encouraging fostering to try to reduce the number of children in residential care, of whom, currently, there are about 250. The board has established a fostering and adoption team, whose team leader's salary will be paid by NCH Action For Children for three years. In the first year forty children left residential for foster care. Now the organization has turned its attention to a demonstration project to place children with physical disabilities or learning difficulties in foster care. This is a new concept in Barbados; NCH Action For Children works closely with the board, which will take over the project if the initial three-year experimental period proves successful. In Barbados, too, a children's development centre has been established, bringing together a wide number of departments, from NCH Action For Children and elsewhere, to serve children. In St Vincent there is also a children's development centre, albeit more modest in scope, exclusively run by NCH Action For Children.

In Grenada the government approached the agency partly to ask for help with traumatized young people after the US invasion in 1983. Vivienne Coombe, a development worker, was appointed and did much to help set up a broad-based Council of Child Welfare, which both carries out educational programmes and influences government policy. A Council for the Disabled was also set up, and training programmes were begun for staff in residential homes and day nurseries run by the government and other voluntary bodies. When her work for NCH ended, Vivienne Coombe was appointed chief welfare officer with continued support from the agency. In Grenada NCH Action For Children also employs a fostering and adoption officer. At Tufton Hall, a centre for boys, providing both residential and day care, it pays the salary of the project leader and offers other financial and professional support.

One of the most successful examples of the organization's overseas work is to be found in Dominica. There has been an active collaboration between the organization and the government where money from the former has been used for 'seeding', to develop a range of services. Work began on the island with funding for a facility for street boys, and both day care and a residential project were set up. The government gradually took over the running of the project, which is now a independent non-government organization.

NCH Action For Children's work then expanded to develop a project for sexually abused children and training for foster-parents. The government took the original funding but the agency is paying for its expansion. The latest venture will be work with disabled children with a view to, again, the government finally assuming the costs.

In Belize the plight of teenage girls seemed the most urgent of the Central American country's social problems. Many of those most at risk finished their schooling at twelve. They drifted into street life with its dangers of drugs and prostitution. A project to help them was partly funded by the British government's aid wing, the Overseas Development Administration. It offers counselling and remedial education, and teaches the girls basic skills to enhance their chances of finding a job. Some of those who attend are mothers who have spent time on the streets and engaged in prostitution and drug abuse. Most are aged between twelve and fifteen. Again, the project's management has been switched to local people. As a result of the project's success two more projects have begun. In 1994 a new NCH Action For Children project, aimed at the increasing problem of teenage pregnancy, was established in Belize.[3]

The Caribbean is not the only focus for NCH Action For Children's overseas work. In Zimbabwe its standing is different from that elsewhere. It has a long-standing relationship with the Matthew Rusike Home, a Methodist Church home, near Harare. An NCH Action For Children staff member visits twice a year for training purposes and is also involved in other residential child care training throughout the country. From time to time, staff of Matthew Rusike Home have visited the Highbury headquarters for training.

The work in Zimbabwe began in 1950 when a young girl was picked up by what were then the Rhodesian police near the small town of Muuma. She was filthy and starving and had been scavenging among the refuse. When no relative could be found, she was handed by the Salisbury police commissioner to the Rev. Matthew Rusike, a Methodist minister, who took her into his home and cared for her. She had been one of three children born to an alcoholic father and mother who had subsequently left her husband. The girl and her sister had decided to leave home to look for their mother. On their journey they had met a lorry driver who had claimed to know where their mother was. But he had driven off with the older sister, abandoning the younger by the roadside. She had never seen the driver or her sister again. A few months after the girl came into the care of Mr Rusike, another was brought to him. She had been sold by her stepmother to a village N'Anga, a spirit medium or witch doctor. He had used her for 'medical experiments'. Her cries were heard by a police-man, who rescued her.

In time other children came. Today the Home cares for eighty of them.[4] Matthew Rusike's enterprise began in circumstances that Thomas Bowman Stephenson would have recognized. He did not found an organization which became as widespread as Stephenson's and it was never a branch of the UK organization. The relationship between the two is more a fraternal one, the larger body offering advice and assistance when required.

The relationship between NCH Action For Children and its overseas partners has, though, not been one-way. Lessons have been learnt on the British side. The issues of race have indicated the need for new sensitivities in the Caribbean as in the UK, and undertaking social work in so many different kinds of places has had much to teach those in the UK: the need to rely on community resources and volunteers; to work as a small team in a large community; to adapt and modify limited resources and material; to develop patchwork community teams; to meet the problems of communications between islands; and to run relevant training programmes with limited resources.

More negatively, in the words of the former (British) regional co-ordinator in the East Caribbean:

> *The effect of colonialism and neo-colonialism means there is still a tendency for many Caribbean people to underestimate and undervalue their own talents and resources, and to look outside for the answers. For example, social work students often apply immediately to North America or Britain for further training after their courses, thereby negating their local training.*[5]

In Zimbabwe, by contrast, there was never any danger of social care colonization: the Harare home began independently and NCH Action For Children's role remains one of consultancy. In Jamaica and the East Caribbean, though the intention was always to employ local staff, this was not always possible. Staff came from other nearby islands or were British expatriates. For some years now in Jamaica all staff have been nationals. The director and deputy director of its work there have, at NCH Action For Children's instigation, had further training on Bristol University's advanced residential course.

Working with local partners—indigenous agencies or the national governments, or by funding staff salaries—has been part of the NCH Action For Children strategy. Where that has not proved possible, it starts its works with the intention of establishing a local agency eventually to continue the work. This has ensured that NCH Action For Children has never been an imposed outsider. And a gradual change in appointments over the years now ensures that no expatriate staff are employed in its overseas work. Indeed, in Jamaica the umbilical cord was loosened even more when in January 1989 the new NCH Jamaica Trust (registered in Jamaica and with a constitution modelled on its UK counterpart) has assumed total responsibility for the work. Funding is continuing at previous levels but it is hoped that within ten years, it will become completely independent.

Considering its overall budget, NCH Action For Children's financial allocation to all its overseas work has been inevitably modest compared with its expenditure in the UK. In 1994/95 it plans to spend £347,700, which will range from £91,200 in Jamaica to £16,600 in St Vincent. (The smallest sum spent overseas will be £9,200 in Zimbabwe.)[6] But these costs will decrease as the UK body ceases, under the new management arrangements, to be responsible for the regional office and the salaries of UK-based staff no longer fall on that part of its balance sheet.[7] But the impact of NCH Action

For Children's work on small and relatively compact island communities has been far greater than the sums might suggest.

The responsibilities taken by local management have still to be tested. But the need for flexibility and adaptability, the desired hallmarks of modern social work wherever it is practised, suggests, as Virginia Membrey wrote,[8] that there continues to remain a role for a voluntary agency in countries and circumstances very different from those in which they first took root.

9 | Twelve projects

From the first children's home in a converted stable in 1869 to a national organization with international links in 1994, NCH Action For Children's growth in provision has diversified with the move away from residential care. So while it continues to offer specialist residential facilities, it also meets the needs of families, young offenders, homeless youngsters and those leaving care, disabled children and many others. Today, in 1994, there are 215 projects in Britain. This chapter looks at twelve very different projects which illustrate the professional and geographical breadth of the organization's work.

BRISTOL

The Bristol Housing Project

Thomas Bowman Stevenson would have seen it as one of his own. Bristol's neat, Edwardian terraced streets camouflage the Bristol Housing Project's three houses, home to thirteen young people. True, he wouldn't recognize the pay telephone or the rooms *en suite*, but the informal, intimate atmosphere has more in common with his re-creation of family living in the first home in Bonner Road than the stately orphanages set in farmland that for nearly a century were NCH's face to the world. There is also another feature of this independent living venture that marks it out from similar NCH Action For Children schemes but which, un-consciously, harks back to the past. For Stephenson's 'housemother' and 'housefather', read 'resident adult'. Each of the three houses has a young adult, who may have been in situations similar to the youngsters with whom they work, who lives rent free and receives an honorarium.

The 'residential adult' is part of the philosophical foundations of the project. It is about much more than giving young people, aged sixteen and over, a roof over their heads, necessary though that is. As Alan Harwood, project leader, puts it, it is about giving the residents an adult they can trust. A qualified social worker and residential worker, Harwood developed the project from an embryonic leaving care initiative that was part of a children's home that closed. He says that the youngsters with whom he works are fed up with many social workers, and social work in general. The resident adults, some of whom may be thinking of a career in youth, community or social work, are, importantly, not NCH Action For Children staff members (the honorarium, he stresses, is not a salary). Their task is a mixture of the practical and the emotional: to befriend, but also to see the house is clean; and to advise, but also to say when the music is too loud.

Alan Harwood cannot pretend that he is not a social worker but he tries not to act like one. He keeps the regimes of the houses as informal as possible—the last thing their residents want is to see the project as an extension of the local authority care which may have dictated their experience of life so far.

'What I hope to provide is an adult they can trust', says Alan Harwood. 'That's something they may never have had. Most youngsters who live at home have a parent or parents they can trust. But we've got youngsters who have never lived at home or who are estranged from their parents. Our aim is to give them the opportunity to make their own decisions against a background of advice from adults they can trust.'

The project has responded to what its residents want it to be. Everything has to be in the open. Honesty with the young people is a key word. For example, if they do something of which their social worker should be informed, they are asked to tell the social worker. If they don't, then they are told that Alan Harwood or Gill Jackman, the part-time project worker and only other member of staff, will have a duty to do so.

'If I am angry with them,' says Alan Harwood, 'I tell them so.' If there is a decision to be taken that affects other residents, then those other residents have to be consulted; like the time when one of them wanted a cat, for example. Learning to live with others is perhaps the most important skill to master and disputes are the most frequent reason why residents come together. But it is not for staff to resolve a dispute by taking a decision; they may mediate or chair a meeting around the kitchen table. It's a dispute between the youngsters and the youngsters have to resolve it.

The project began in 1987. NCH Action For Children owns two of the houses, which it leases back to a housing association, and the third house is owned by another housing association. Money to finance the project comes from the housing associations through Avon social services department (which also provides social work support), the Housing Corporation, Bristol's housing department, and residents' rents (usually met from housing benefit). From the beginning the need was to take youngsters with different backgrounds: to take only those who were in care or who had been in care might replicate the only system they knew.

'I'm trying to break a dependency that some of the young people have on social services,' says Alan Harwood. 'I'm trying to get them to live independently and not depend on seeing a social worker each week.'

The average length of stay in the houses is about eighteen months though it may last as little as a few weeks, or as long as two-and-a-half years. When the youngsters leave, the hope is that they are equipped with skills to negotiate with the official bodies who may be a part of their lives—social security, the social services department, the employment office. What it is most difficult to equip them with—and it has become more so even in the seven years of the project's existence—is a home and a job. Housing is difficult but employment even more so. For some, their futures may be with friends. If they have learned to live in the project's houses they will have learned to live with others. Some of them may secure council housing. Yet others may go to housing associations catering especially for single people.

For young women who become pregnant, accommodation, other than from the local authority, is extremely difficult to find. They face the greatest struggle to make their way in the world, and to find a reasonable income and decent accommodation. It is they who easily find themselves back in the web of reliance on different agencies. They may not have escaped the 'dependency culture' but, hopefully, their time with the project will have taught them the skills to find their way through that web.

If those with them the project works who find some kind of satisfactory accommodation are in the majority, it is a small minority who find a job. Even youth training opportunities are drying up. In times of job scarcity employers can be choosy and many youngsters do not come from backgrounds where the disciplines, even the understanding, of work come easily. They may not always turn up on time; they may not turn up at all. They may come from homes where their parents were unemployed. What does it mean to go out to work? They may have been in local authority care where people go on and off duty, not go out to work at regular times.

To come to live in one of the houses, potential residents must be in work or seeking it (which the Department of Social Security insists on); be willing to make agreements and stick to them; take on responsibility to look after themselves (they must have an income); and contribute to the running of the house. Loud music after 11 p.m. is not allowed; there must not be drugs on the premises; guests are allowed to stay but residents are asked to let the resident adult or staff know; excessive drinking is discouraged. Tough rules for some youngsters. Inevitably, there have been occasional incidents where some residents have stolen from other residents or threatened resident adults with violence.

Eviction, admits Alan Harwood, feels like an admission of failure. No one is evicted without somewhere to go. But such a step must be seen in the young person's long-term interests, even if they don't see it like that at the time. Stephen, for example, not a drug user himself, moved in circles where drugs were used. Too often half a dozen outside friends could be found in his room. They were using it as a safe place to take their drugs. He wasn't able to tell them they couldn't. He went, but today he meets staff in the city, he has moved away from his drug-using friends, and he bears the project no ill will.

Tracy never had any difficulty in finding and keeping jobs. But at seventeen she decided she wanted to 'become a housewife' but had to leave the project as she couldn't set up home in a project house. She moved in with a boyfriend, paying no rent but having to offer services, probably sexual as well as practical, in the house to him and others. She saw the situation she had got into. She left and found a bedsit. When Alan Harwood saw her, visiting a friend still living in the project, she had two jobs and said having to leave had been the best thing for her. It had forced her to put some order in her life.

Jimmy wanted to stay away from the project with friends every other night. Alan Harwood said he'd prefer to see him at the house but he could only give him advice, not orders. For Jimmy it was a hard lesson to learn. He returned only after he had been attacked and robbed.

'A lot of young people are going to make mistakes,' says Alan Harwood. 'They will have to learn from them. We all do. Our youngsters are the ones who make more mistakes but they learn more than most.'

The names of the young people have been changed.

CALDERDALE

The Calderdale Leaving Care Project

In the beginning there was only the room. Nothing more. The premises which the local authority were to provide under the joint project were never used. They were totally unsuitable. A local Methodist Church came to the rescue with the room, but for a project set up to help young people leaving local authority care, where was the space to talk quietly? Staff supervision was held in the local coffee bar.

Seven years later the Calderdale Council/NCH Action For Children Leaving Care Project is housed in a pleasant dark brick building in a small residential street in the centre of Halifax. There is room for counselling, and relaxation and activities are available for the young people who treat it very often as the family home they never had.

But a change of premises is not the only thing to have changed since 1987. Starting from scratch, the team—it now consists of a project manager, two full-time project workers, a part-timer, and volunteers—had little to go on. The estimates about how many young people would want to use such a service were thrown awry even by early experience.

Today, too, the needs of young people leaving care may seem self-evident—decent housing, some kind of income, a sympathetic ear, occasional practical help—but Calderdale Council's first attempts to assist got off on a wrong footing. Housing applications to the authority gathered dust until a social worker inquired about progress. And when accommodation was found by the council, youngsters found themselves in bleak high-rise blocks that nobody else wanted to live in. Communication between social workers and housing may have been the problem but getting accommodation, no matter how poor, was seen as the solution. An accommodation officer, Fran Orford (who is now the project's leader) was appointed.

Calderdale Council had shown an understanding of the total needs of young people in its care. Its first attempt to do something about that was a paper in 1984, which Fran Orford wrote. In it he talked of the 'inadequate preparation' that the experience of care offered for life outside. The paper also remarked on the lack of support for care leavers, and problems in finding jobs and housing. It recognized that for some young people 'their first experiences of independent living are traumatic'.[1]

The paper also said that 'no real policy existed in Calderdale ... each residential home deals with this issue on an *ad hoc* basis'. Fran Orford went on: 'My feeling is that preparation for leaving care at any worthwhile level is a hit or miss affair poorly planned and poorly resourced.' There were few hard facts as to what happened to the youngsters in Calderdale but 'the problems that result from this lack of preparation have been researched in other parts of the country, [and] there is no reason to believe that these same problems are not being experienced there.'

At this point Calderdale responded to an NCH offer of help funded by the sale of property, with other funding offered from NCH centrally. But the kind of project needed, given the false start of creating an accom-modation officer post, emerged only slowly by drawing together everyone with an interest (including the young people). Ideas like 'home builders' (teaching practical skills like cookery and ironing) were rejected—they were only a part of the whole service needed—while 'half-way houses' between care and independence could too easily become another form of institutional care.

Funding today's project was struck upon with an even sharing of costs between the council and the organization, but looking to a time when the council would bear them all. Today, NCH Action For Children meets management costs and owns the house, while Calderdale's bill is 80 per cent of the annual £100,000 running costs, in addition to which it gives leaving care grants.

At any one time about ninety young people are being helped—nearly half of them living in tenancies secured by the project, thirty managing on their own with some involvement, and about twenty occasionally using the project. They are some of the 400 youngsters whom the project has worked with since it began.

In big cities, young people (and often those who have been in care) can drift among the homeless, sheltering in doorways. Calderdale is a small authority with a population of 190,000 and Halifax is its biggest town. Yet every one of the care leavers whom the project has worked with (and that is 90 per cent of them) lives or will live in good quality accommodation. The local authority gives them high priority on its waiting list, but half of the homes come through the six housing associations with whom the project works. It has a special partnership with one, Sanctuary, which gives the project a number of allocations each year. But for youngsters waiting for a home of their own (which often might be a newly refurbished one-person flat) or who do not yet feel able to take the plunge into full independence, the project recruits local families to offer 'supported accommodation', paid for by Housing Benefit.

Most of the young people don't have jobs. This seems to worry them less than might be thought, but their aspirations, at a time of recession and mass unemployment, have been whittled away. Most of their friends are unemployed and they often come from families where a job is the exception. Youth Training Schemes often offer little real training and no prospect of a job afterward. YTS allowances have not been reviewed for seven years and are now less than Income Support for eighteen-year-olds.

The young people's launch into independence is helped considerably by Calderdale's generous leaving care grants. There is no national minimum payment for young adults leaving care. Some local authorities pay as little as £50; Calderdale's £1,200 is the third highest in the country[2]. Calderdale also tops up benefit at an average of £20 for each youngster in their own tenancy and involved in some kind of further education or training. Most youngsters seem to get by—the ending of single payments through the social security system and the stopping of benefit for sixteen- to eighteen-year-olds has been cushioned by Calderdale's generosity. For the rest there's a buoyant black economy. Crime and pushing drugs have risen since the social security changes in 1987 and the deepening of unemployment among young people, filling for some what would otherwise be empty pockets.

Counselling is also a part of the project's work—a social security query; a new relationship; occasional despair at where life is leading (or not leading); problems resulting from drugs or gambling. Volunteers are often used as befrienders but one of them, Ken Smith, who was himself in care and later became a paid project worker, says: 'I don't like the term. You are either a friend or you aren't.' When a volunteer is not chewing over a problem, he or she might be off on holiday at Centreparcs, going away with one or two youngsters, or involved in activities at the house (table tennis, badminton and netball are on offer, rug making and cooking have been), or helping someone move house—when care makes you totally dependent, even buying a TV or some cups and saucers may seem daunting.

Fran Orford puts the project's success down to a number of factors: Calderdale's smallness as an authority helps communications and NCH Action For Children is an independent body able to advocate on a youngster's behalf, as well as strike deals with other agencies in a way that a statutory, bureaucratized body like a local authority can't always do. He also says that the culture of the work is different: 'The Pavlovian reaction of a social services department is that work with care leavers needs social work and a social worker. Our first staff members, apart from me, had been in care themselves. It made all the difference in shaping what we did and how we did it. They knew what was needed from their experience. We saw we needed to set up a system. We saw accommodation was the big problem—the right kind of accommodation, accommodation the youngsters wanted in areas in which they wanted to live—and we set about getting it. I know of agencies still who say "We haven't got accommodation" but they aren't doing anything about it.'

But while youngsters may often be in crisis, the project is not a crisis service. Fran Orford again: 'Too many agencies say "When you've got a problem come and see us." We say "Yes, come and see us," too, but also "Come and see us when you've got a new boyfriend or girlfriend." We've lots of young mothers and parents among those we work with and we'll be among the first in the hospital with the flowers to celebrate the birth.'

Many young women with whom the project works either are pregnant, have had a child or have had a termination. Most will be sexually active by the time they come in contact with the project. A mixture of ignorance and a reluctance to use contraceptives aggravates the situation of many. Some of the young women, however, have now decided that they'd like to visit children's homes to talk about the negative experiences of too early motherhood—not being able to go out, sleepless nights, tight purses further tightened—to other young women in care.

Few of the young women have partners who play any role in the child's upbringing. The Child Support Agency, set up by the government to chase up fathers who aren't contributing financially to their children's welfare, brings in its trail added problems for Calderdale's young parents. Mothers risk losing benefit if they do not reveal the names of the father, and fathers, if found, will have to dig deeper into their already meagre finances. For both parents the poverty trap tightens its grip.

One result of the project's work is that expectations have risen. Young people don't now expect to be shunted into accommodation that no one else wants and thus they have less reason to go off and try their own hand and possibly come to grief. Another thing is that the prospect that everyone will get good quality accommodation means that some workers working with youngsters still in care find it easy to find ways to help them manage their problems before they leave—and few leave at sixteen, most at seventeen, and some are over eighteen.

'When they come here,' says Ken Smith 'they feel like they are coming into a family, even though they may be as apprehensive as any one else facing change. They know that someone does love them, someone cares.'

But, as Fran Orford says, the project can never be more than a small, if significant part in the youngsters' lives. For many that's enough. For others in crisis, with a family that is not always there, an abyss can beckon.

CORNWALL

The Share Youth Counselling Project

The beginning was not the most auspicious. Six weeks after Jan Goudge joined the newly established Cornwall Share Youth Counselling Project as its co-ordinator in 1990, with hopes for modest expansion, the county council's youth service—partners with NCH Action For Children—cut its grant from £69,000 to £26,000. Plans for six co-ordinators throughout the county had to be scrapped and the administrative worker's hours fell by four-fifths to five hours a week.

Four years later the demands on the service continue to grow but Jan Goudge remains the only full-time salaried employee. She herself works as a counsellor, as well as supervising the eighteen volunteer counsellors, and takes part (with the sessionally employed trainer) in the training they are given. The service is for those aged fourteen to twenty-five and covers the whole of Cornwall. Some youngsters who contact the service may want no more than practical advice, or have a problem nagging at them, perhaps to do with housing. They may be helped by Cornwall's Share Information and Advice service (partners in the counselling service), which is often the first port of call for would-be clients. But those needing counselling embark on what may be a course of sessions lasting several months or, occasionally, a year to eighteen months.

Clients come for a variety of reasons: sexual abuse; problems with relationships; a feeling that life lacks value (making them potentially suicidal); school and college problems; isolation or homelessness. Seventy per cent of the young people (the service is for those aged fourteen to twenty-five) will have been sexually abused, although their original reason for contact may be something else entirely and only later do they reveal their abuse.

Rural areas have particular problems—poor communications, isolation, unemployment, low pay, a lack of affordable housing. Young people tend to stay in the family home for longer than average. Cornwall stretches for a hundred miles from Launceston to Penzance. If young people want to see a counsellor it is much less easy to make contact than if they were living in a city or a town. The Share Project can be contacted through its own office in Bodmin or the information and advice centres and county youth service offices in St Austell, Camborne and Truro, as well through family centres, health centres, and GPs' surgeries. For those who do not find these easily accessible, there is a county-wide freephone and counsellors will visit youngsters near where they are, rather than expecting them to find a way of getting to a counselling centre.

The counselling project is a confidential service—except in the case of disclosed child abuse. The confidentiality rule can cause problems. Some schools feel an obligation to tell parents if a child wants to see a counsellor, even though the young person may not want this. Other schools are more flexible and will not only observe confidentiality but will give pupils time off to see the counsellor. Some pupils' ability to see a counsellor may rely on the restricting schedule of the school bus—and home itself may be a mile or so down a track from the bus stop. Jan Goudge has counselled on the top deck of the youth service bus in a car park.

Sixty-five per cent of those who come to Share are young women, from the entire age-range, fourteen to twenty-five. The young men tend to be aged mostly between fifteen and eighteen. The difference can perhaps be explained by the respective abilities of the sexes to talk about feelings. 'It is not a macho thing for the boys to talk about feelings,' says Jan Goudge. 'When I went to a school to talk about the service I asked pupils whether they would go to a counsellor. The boys said that you really had to be desperate, the girls thought it was OK. Also, in a farming community, stereotypes are reinforced or created by the tendency to allow roles according to gender: "This is your job, and this is yours." '

Counselling services, from Childline to the Samaritans to pastoral staff in schools, are not difficult to come by. What, then, makes Share different? Does its existence indicate a failure on the part of teachers or parents? First, teachers are not primarily counsellors, though some may have a specific pastoral responsibility. Second, some youngsters are estranged from their families (parents may not even be aware that youngsters are attending the service, even when they have contact with them). But also, parents may be too close to the young person, there may be too many associations in that relationship to allow the openness and honesty that counselling gives. Share is complementary, providing what others cannot.

The Share Youth Counselling Project has an open-handed approach to the clients. It prefers young people to make their own contact but many are referred by GPs, social services, schools, youth centres, even parents. The project will only see those who want to be seen, and for those who do come there is a choice of a male or female counsellor. Youngsters who have drink or drug problems will usually be referred to the county council's specialist drug and alcohol service.

Share requires much of its voluntary counsellors. While each counsellor offers three counselling hours a week, at the same time they must have one-and-a-half hours individual supervision a month and two hours group supervision, as well as training. Counsellors have to be willing to examine their self-awareness as they will not be able to help a client if they have unresolved conflicts. For example, a counsellor would have difficulty in assisting someone through the stages of bereavement if he or she had not come to terms with a personal bereavement.

All of this may seem such a commitment one might expect a rapid turnover, but, in fact, since the project began, only three counsellors have left. All counsellors have a diploma, certificate or substantial experience in counselling or have worked in a field, like teaching, with pastoral experience and training. This may seem to restrict volunteers greatly in terms of their background and experience. But despite what it seems the requirement is not restrictive. One of the volunteers is a dairy farmer, who is also a qualified masseur and holds a counselling certificate from Exeter University—acquired before he ever joined the project.

Share's name reflects its belief that the essence of the service is the relationship between client and counsellor and a concentration on the quality of that relationship, from which help and healing can flow. This approach encourages clients to make their own decisions, to seek their own solutions, and make the changes in their lives which may be needed. Counsellors are not there to advise, judge or criticize, nor to direct, however unintentionally, a client into what may seem to be the 'best' alternative or solution. The aim is to create a relationship based on warmth, empathy, trust, respect and genuineness.

The approach is one which Share calls 'client-centred' and 'non-directive'. It is based on a belief that human beings are basically capable of moving in a positive direction. Through openness they learn to trust themselves (and others). The aim is to help the client feel respected and safe, and so be helped in a way which opens up new possibilities for their lives. This allows them to go beyond the illusions and defences which they may have constructed in order to prevent them facing the reality of their lives. This can be painful. Moving in this direction must be done at the client's pace.

Jan Goudge says: 'Counselling has the potential for change but also for damage, which is why supervision is so important. We have to know what is achievable with clients, so counselling is very much about negotiating, contracting, finding what the client wants and going at their rate—you can't make someone grieve faster, for example.'

The counsellor helps the client to see what is going on in his or her relationships so that they can relate more openly with people, be more honest, see how much they can trust people. The relationship between counsellor and client is also non-judgmental, something else the client may not have previously experienced. Counselling is about empowering young people, and even if many things in their lives are beyond their control, it gives them the confidence to claim their rights, to seek help, to go on to further education or training.

Take the case of Sue (not her real name), who came to Share when she was seventeen, having been sexually abused by her grandfather over a period of ten years. She had already, unsuccessfully, sought the help of educational and clinical psychologists, a psychiatrist and a worker at a family centre. For her, Share was a last-ditch attempt to find help at a time when she was feeling suicidal and there was no one to help. Her previous sources of help had been unable to deal with their own feelings in finding out about her situation. At first she found it difficult to talk at Share, but Sue grew to trust the counsellor to deal with what she was telling her and to trust herself.

Sue had found it difficult to talk to her mother in the face of her grandfather's threats: he said he would kill her mother, and she would be sent away. He had bribed her with money. There had been an ambivalence in his attitude toward her: she was special but what he was doing to her was all she deserved; she was no more than a sexual object. Later, when he was dying of cancer, she felt unable to tell anyone what had happened.

Sue was counselled for several months, during which time she talked not only about her grandfather and the abuse but also about current relationships, such as her parents' marriage breaking up and her relationship with her boyfriend. She came to understand the effect which abuse had had on her, and particularly on her relationship with men. For her, counselling has been helpful but, she says, the most difficult thing was attending the sessions, even though she knew they were helping.

Today, with so much pain in her past, life offers Sue the chance of change for the better: a place at university, a new stepmother, her mother's new partner, moving house, and the possibility of a new counsellor at university. There remain areas in her life of which she needs to take control. Share has helped, but Sue also knows that having a boyfriend who has demonstrated his love and is still there, even when things are difficult, has enhanced the healing, not least because now she can talk to him about the abuse and her feelings.

And how do other clients respond to what the service offers them? One young woman, who had suffered a traumatic bereavement, settled at university, and wrote to Share:

> I really want to thank you for your support and for listening.
> . . . Sometimes I think it is not worth going on without him. I don't
> know what would have happened to me if I hadn't been able to talk
> to you . . . You've helped me to think about the future, though I
> thought I didn't have one.

EXETER

The Beacon Heath Family Centre

For Selina Nicholas—abused in her own childhood, having been to fourteen children's homes, and now four months pregnant with her fifth child while her partner is in prison—it is the place of safety, which she has always sought. Tracey McCartney, a single parent with two children, says that before she came here she had no enthusiasm for anything, and, unable to talk to her parents, had no one in whom she could confide. Amber Griffiths, abused by her father and now on her own with two children, finds it somewhere where she can trust people, where staff 'don't go behind your back'.

To the casual observer there is no obvious deprivation on the Beacon Heath Estate. Shops are not boarded up, there are no empty houses, or run-down properties; there are no abandoned, burned-out cars on scruffy grass verges. It is a few miles from Exeter city centre, with well-kept houses, clean streets, shops, schools and playing fields. But in an area where two-thirds of homes are owner-occupied, there are the hidden statistics that say that life is not all it could be for a substantial number of those who live there. A third of households have children aged nought to fifteen years, 22 per cent are headed by single parents, of whom half have children under five. 65 per cent of all parents are not in paid work, 18 per cent work part-time and only 14 per cent are employed full-time. Male unemployment is 8 per cent but 20 per cent of men are only in part time work. 75 per cent of women are either not at work or in part-time jobs.

When the Beacon Heath Family Centre, which Selina, Amber, Tracey and their children attend, opened in September 1990, it was in response to poor social provision. The estate—and its associated housing areas of Stoke Hill and parts of Whipton—had grown rapidly. Many of the new residents had previously been in bed and breakfast accommodation, the families were young, children small. Yet there was virtually nothing for children under five, not even a child health clinic.

Lobbying by councillors brought funding from NCH, Devon social services, education, and housing departments, and the local health authority, and when it opened in September 1990 the project came managerially under NCH's wing.

The centre is situated in what was a detached private house, opposite shops, indistinguishable from the houses either side, except for the NCH

Action For Children logo. It is very much a part of the local area. This is not just because it looks like it does. It is also because of what it is. It is an 'open' family centre: anyone with children—parents, foster-parents, child-minders—can use it. Some centres take only 'referrals': families whose main problems are child abuse and the primary concern is child protection. They may well offer the same range of services as Beacon Heath provides—parent and baby group, play sessions, housing advice, counselling, a baby clinic, a women's group, a summer club, baby equipment loans, outings, the chance to meet others—but in the eyes of neighbours those attending may be marked out as 'problem families'. And while social services departments run open family centres, the very fact that they come under the statutory services may help to label those who use them.

Eighty families use the centre, though only three or four men are among the parents who come. Some parents have terrible histories of being abused themselves. Some live in poverty, are divorced, or have never been married. Others come from stable marriages. Some women have partners in prison, one man is a prison officer; many women are on their own, one woman is a vicar's wife. Some women walk to the centre because they cannot afford the bus fare, one comes in the family's second car.

There is a very explicit anti-discriminatory stance to the place. As the women themselves wrote in the bright information pack which they put together: 'Our centre is welcoming and friendly. We provide time and space for parents and a stimulating environment for children as well as a range of community facilities. We are aware that some parents feel excluded from such services because they will be in a minority (for example, male carers, people with disabilities or people of a different race or religion). There are no exclusions here; we welcome everyone, and will try to ensure our provision is appropriate to your needs.' (There is wheelchair access to the ground floor.) The centre recognizes that some users will be racist or sexist, and if so this is challenged 'constructively', as project leader Sally Randall puts it.

But Beacon Heath and others like it do not dodge the fact that parents can do dreadful things to their children. Project worker Maria McLaughlin explains: 'We are not stigmatizing like social services, so people find it very easy to come here. But we don't run away from child protection. When we suspect it or know about it we have to work on it. We have to talk to the parent first and, if need be, involve social services. But we never go behind parents' backs.'

It is not unknown for parents who have injured their children to come to the centre and say so and ask for help. That help may be counselling, help with parenting skills, respite care (where the centre and the social services department find somewhere else for the child to go for a break), or for the parent to have the child taken into voluntary care. Staff will attend case conferences with parents. There have been occasions when the centre has taken an initiative whereby children have been taken compulsorily into the care of the local authority. But that has yet to mean that a parent has ceased, in anger or despair, to attend.

Staffed by one full-time project leader (on a job share), one full time project worker, a part-time play leader and secretary, as well as volunteers and parent helpers, like Tracey McCartney, user participation has a high priority at Beacon Heath. Meetings are regular but informal. Those who use the centre do not run it—they do not fix budgets, say how the budget will be divided, or appoint staff—but they do say how budgets marked out for different activities will be spent and decide what activities will be undertaken.

The opinions of the users are actively sought by those—staff or funders—who have control over other matters. Two user representatives sit on the management group which comprises representatives from the funding bodies and staff. Matters where users have a say include reviewing with staff the centre's groups and planning new ones. Users also go with staff when talks are given locally about the centre to put across their experiences of using it. Users will also identify areas of unmet need and, with back-up from the centre, develop their own responses. Examples of this have been the setting up of a parent and toddler group on the estate, and a summer club for five- to eight-year-olds.

Project leader Sally Randall says that this is realistic. 'We have always been open about the constraints that exist. As staff we are constrained by our funders and their expectations, as well as by our own expectations, and the users work within that framework.'

It is easy to explain the activities of a family centre. Looking at photographs of activities pinned on walls, the play equipment, the posters and racks of information, no one would mistake it for other than for what it is. But family centre enthusiasts claim that these activities—valuable in themselves—can lead to other things, too: greater self-confidence and self-esteem, the stimulation of support and self-help and better relationships between parent and child. Do they? Tracey McCartney, feeling isolated and lacking motivation to do anything beyond caring for her children at home, says she is now more self-confident. As a result of going to the women's group, she started thinking about the needs of her older child, and began a group for five- to eight-year-olds, which she now runs. She works in the centre and she is about to embark on a two-year Pre-School Playgroups Association training scheme.

Selina Nicholas' life has been marked by hardship. Her father was a criminal, her mother abandoned her and went to the United States with two of her sisters leaving Selina and another sister in care. She had been abused by her father, a family friend, and in a children's home. She had been expelled from school and violence against staff had brought her through the courts. At ten she was being dosed with Largactil. 'I never had a chance to understand my own feelings, to learn how to deal with my problems.' Today she admits that drink is the easiest way for her to deal with problems.

She had attended a number of other family centres, none of which met her needs. At Beacon Heath she has had counselling and been a member of two women's groups. Even as a child, she'd always written poetry ('I love words. I wake up sometimes at two in the morning and jot down rhymes.') She has not only been encouraged to write at the centre but has attended a writers' group with three or four other women and now has hopes of having her work published. Some of her poems are on the centre's walls.

Selina is only one of the women Maria McLaughlin is talking about when she says: 'People who have so much need also have a lot to offer and that is something that a centre like this picks up.' Selina herself says: 'Staff here work beside you. In other centres it felt like they worked mainly for the children. Here it feels like it's for the family and kids. It's supportive. It's solid, something to fall back on in whatever you are going through.'

Amber Griffiths says that the women's group allowed her to understand that she was not alone in her feelings and problems; Tracey McCartney felt she could be listened to and not criticized.

'The world always seems a bit creepy to me', so far as Selina Nicholas is concerned. 'Six years ago I nearly lost my life. Now,' she says, 'it feels safe here.'

GLASGOW

The San Jai Project

Mrs Chan's life says as much about the problems of being an elderly Chinese woman in the middle of Glasgow as the House of Commons' Home Affairs committee had to say about her community in its report of three volumes in 1985.[1] She comes through the doors of the San Jai Project in the city's Garnetthill area, an unpaid council tax bill in her hand. She cannot understand English. What can she do? Who will help her? This is not her first call and it will not be her last. This problem, at least, is easily dealt with by one of the project's three workers.

Mrs Chan has come before, often for the most apparently trivial reasons. Dorothy Neoh, project leader, sees Mrs Chan's frequent visits as a way of living out the grief caused by her husband's death. Three months before, when Dorothy Neoh first joined the project, Mrs Chan introduced herself with the words: 'I am the woman whose husband has died.'

The Home Affairs committee, which devoted a section of its report especially to Scotland, where the Chinese are the second largest ethnic minority after the Asian community, said that the Chinese faced greater difficulties than other groups. They were particularly disadvantaged by lack of awareness about their rights, by non-use of services (of whose existence they were often not even aware), and by language difficulties.

The report's publication coincided with the birth of the San Jai Project, the brainchild of Zara Ross, then NCH's Scottish development officer. Originally funded by the Urban Aid programme, with money from the Scottish Office channelled through Strathclyde Regional Council, its £60,000 annual budget (which has nearly doubled in eight years), is now divided equally between NCH Action For Children and the Strathclyde Regional Council.

Its present home, attractively decorated small premises with meeting rooms and offices, stands on the 'small hill', which gives the project its Chinese name. The area rises gently above the busy city centre shopping area, only minutes from the main thoroughfare of Sauchiehall Street. Garnetthill is part of the expanding Glaswegian Chinatown. It is a typical inner city street: handsome sandstone terraces give way to new, low-rise redbrick flats; anti-poll tax posters still decorate the wall of a newly created playground, with its sloping lawn and wooden climbing frames. Around the back stands an anonymous Holiday Inn hotel. On the brow of the hill, looking down on all it surveys, is the narrow, dark edifice that is St Aloysius' Church. The Chinese may be the largest ethnic minority group here, but they live cheek by jowl with Poles, Jews and Asians. Along the road is the Garnetthill Multicultural Centre.

There are reckoned to be 1,000 Chinese people in Garnetthill. Exact figures are difficult to come by, but that is a tenth of the Chinese population in the giant Strathclyde region. In Scotland as a whole there are reckoned to be 20,000 Chinese. Most come from Hong Kong, speaking Hakka and Cantonese, and, as with Chinese populations in most places, find work in the restaurant trade, where the hours are long, conditions poor, pay low, and trade unionism non-existent. It is an old-established community—the Chinese started coming to the UK in the last decades of the last century—and the very elderly number between one and two thousand in the region. But, in a community only two or three generations old, people of fifty and sixty age greatly, given the hardship of their lives.

San Jai does not just serve the immediate community. It also offers services to Chinese people elsewhere in Strathclyde. Some of these may live very isolated lives—when perhaps one family runs a take-away in a small rural town where they constitute the only Chinese population. They may not even know of San Jai's existence. The project's resources are so stretched that it can hardly meet the needs of those within the region's borders, let alone step outside them. Yet this is the only Chinese project in Scotland.

San Jai began with one worker and there are now three. Dorothy Neoh, born in Malaysia of Chinese extraction, is a trained social worker, who came to the project after working with the Chinese population at Edinburgh's race equality council. Heather Lee works full time as administration and information worker, and Ezar Monaghan is a project worker.

Dorothy Neoh says that NCH Action for Children is keen on outreach—projects which reach out to those whom they seek to serve—but resources make that less a reality than she would like it to be. So the project enables outreach by other bodies: Rose Street is home to regular sessions on housing advice given by Shelter, the national housing and homelessness charity, and the Citizens Advice Bureau. There are also plans afoot for the health board to set up a clinic in the building, with a Chinese doctor and nurse. Many Chinese people may not know how to register with GPs, let alone seek assistance from other less visible public bodies.

Two days a week there is a crêche run by two local authority staff, and another worker runs the Chinese dance group, much in demand in local cultural events. For youngsters there is an after-school club where they can go until their parents return from work, and now Dorothy Neoh is thinking about a club for youngsters who are under court supervision orders. Once a week the centre hosts English classes.

Behind the three aims of the project—to provide an information, advice and counselling service; empower the community to seek and develop new services; and to make existing resources more accessible—lies the ambition to 'promote self-esteem and status'.

What does this mean in practice, and what are the natural strengths of the community? Dorothy Neoh does not deny the commonly observed communal characteristics of attachment to family, independence and the ethic of self-sufficiency. But she believes that these can also have their negative side. In the mother country these characteristics may have held together centuries of community living in the rural areas from which the majority of the Glaswegian Chinese come, or from where their families originate. But transport those families several thousand miles to a Western city and they can be traits that isolate people: self-sufficiency becomes a reluctance to seek help; family support rules out making use of the welfare state; independence can sit uneasily with taking up one's rights, even if they are known. So for the project, the aim must be to marry self-sufficiency and self-determination with an acceptance of a citizen's rights to services.

But for the Mrs Chans of Garnetthill there is, of course, the danger of encouraging dependence: how easy to do everything for someone who, handicapped by language barriers and the welfare maze, may seem lost. Of this Dorothy Neoh and her colleagues are all too well aware. They want to help but also to instruct. What happens if they aren't available? Mrs Chan and her neighbours have to be assisted to seek help and information on their own. The project workers are anxious to see that other professionals with whom they work—the GPs, the social workers from the local authority, the health visitors and the police—don't see them as only interpreters (valuable as that may be at times). Likewise, the project workers are keen that their clients' fellow Chinese see the project workers as more than the people who help you with a visa or who contact the local tax office with a query.

The other, more demanding problems for which help is sought at the project are often complicated by cultural assumptions that often inform, or even cause, them. Take the single mother with three teenage children. When she attempted to exercise authority over her three teenage sons coming home late at night with girlfriends, they rebelled and she, coming from a background where the parent's word is law, did not know how to react. She went to the project, and here the interweaving relationships within the community offered a possible solution. The mother of one of the boy's girlfriends was herself a user of the service; she, too, was faced with children defiant of her authority. What more natural thing than to bring the two women together?

Or there was the case of Mrs Liu. She woke her teenage daughter in the night and hit her severely with a book as punishment for some transgression. The girl told her teacher, who told the social work department and Mrs Liu ended up with a social worker on her doorstep. Juliet Gallacher, then a project worker, was called in as co-worker. But Mrs Liu's reaction was not to deny that she had beaten her child but to object to her daughter alerting strangers and bringing them to their home. If her daughter thought these white people could help her more than her own mother, then perhaps she should go with them, she said, suggesting that the daughter might be better off in care. These strangers were intervening in a dispute within the family. Mrs Liu saw the chastisement as punishment: after all, who were these people to help? They were unable to discipline their own children, who drank, took drugs and had sex without anyone seeming to care.

Strathclyde social work department decided that it would not apply for a care order. Mrs Liu did not want the social worker in her home again, but she would welcome back Juliet Gallacher—she was, after all, Chinese. She would understand, even if she did not agree. Thus, it was Juliet Gallacher's job to seek reconciliation between mother and daughter and to make Mrs Liu aware that certain kinds of punishment which, as a Chinese person, she might find acceptable, were not acceptable in Britain and that there were consequences for parents who thought otherwise.

This is not to say that Juliet Gallacher sided with Mrs Liu, or that she and her colleagues are on the side of their countrypeople in similar situations. Dorothy Neoh explains: 'We cannot afford to collude with the client. If we took sides we would be no help at all. That problem is always around because there is a cultural and language situation—but just because we are also Chinese doesn't mean we are their friends. But we are also not a part of the social work department; we work in partnership with it. We can speak for the client and with the client. They trust us because we are Chinese and speak their languages.

'In my own heart of hearts I know there are certain ways of doing things—I know how I react and what I expect in my relations with my own mother and how she can speak to me. But with the client I have a different relationship and I must make very clear to them what that is. The Chinese community is very small and everyone knows one another. We have to be detached from that.'

Such attitudes do not mean the imposition of British values on members of the Chinese community, either. The women's group, which meets at the centre, in many ways seems quite traditional: a group of women, making artefacts for sales for local groups, cooking, talking. But these activities may lead to other, more profound things. Chinese women live in a patriarchal society, where men deal with legal and social matters, speak for their partners and are expected to take many initiatives. So women would not take easily to a women's group specifically intended to help them look at their own roles and identities as women, people and citizens. Some women have left their husbands when they have rebelled against traditional roles or found a relationship unacceptable, when their mother, perhaps, might not even have questioned it.

Chinese people do not take easily to discussing their problems in groups, so the project has not made use of conventional forms of group-work, a traditional stronghold of Western social work. It has had to adapt what it does to meet cultural differences. Similarly, helplines would have little use in the project. Opening up one's deepest thoughts, laying bare domestic, emotional or sexual problems to a stranger—especially a non-Chinese stranger—would not be something which a Chinese person would do. And while counselling is offered, it is informal and develops from someone dropping in with another problem. Cruse, the national bereavement service, would be of no help to Mrs Chan, 'the woman whose husband has died', and the prized anonymity of the Samaritans is a positive deterrent to a Chinese person. There is, though, a health group, led by a Chinese-speaking community psychiatric nurse. This has discussed matters such as HIV and AIDS, family planning and domestic violence.

And so San Jai works with those who need its services in a way in which they can accept those services. It is a lively community and a busy project. Someone calls in about a social security query as someone else inquires about the language class, and tomorrow, Dorothy Neoh will go miles to Irvine to meet some Chinese people who have been in touch. If the Commons committee identified real problems for Britain's Chinese people, in Glasgow, after nine years and despite demand outpacing resources, there's every sign that 'the small hill' is ever so slowly being climbed.

Names of people using the project have been changed.

LLANRUMNEY

The Llanrumney Community Project

The Llanrumney estate is like a dozen others to be found from Plymouth to Glasgow, Bath to Birmingham. It is twenty minutes from Cardiff, along dual carriageways lined with DIY and furniture warehouses and the obligatory MacDonalds. In an estate built as the city stretched its borders after the war, the 14,000 inhabitants live in prairies of streets, one much the same as the next, where there is no bank or supermarket, and only two pubs. What passed for a job centre in what is an area of acute unemployment was, until recently, a woman behind a table in the local library. It is a £3 return bus fare to the city centre, a sum to consider, all the more so if you have children and are on social security.

None of this is new to Nigel Billingham, leader of the Llanrumney community project. He came to Llanrumney in 1991, after fifteen years on a sister estate at Ely where he worked for Barnardo's. That estate was built in the 1920s and was also vast, with poor facilities. At one time he was doubling by working for NCH Action For Children on St Mellon's, a new, neighbouring estate. There the facilities are promised. He won't be surprised if they don't appear. What does surprise him is that so little seems to have been learned in forty years.

Nigel Billingham's ambitions are modest. 'It is no good pretending that a community centre, or a small community project like ours, will cure all the problems of a place like Llanrumney,' he says. After all, Llanrumney conforms to stereotypes both in its drab appearance, and also in its statistics: a higher incidence of people living on benefit, a larger number of single parents than the national average. But such figures obscure how much has been achieved since the project's embryonic beginnings in 1979 when a lone NCH worker formed a group for mothers and their small children in a hut in the Glan-yr-Afon School playground. Four years later the hut blew down in a storm. The project, which by this time had acquired a project leader who was shifting it in the direction of community work, moved to new premises above a slightly ramshackle shopping parade and around the corner from the community mural and the graffiti-covered bookmakers shop.

This was not ideal. There was no shopfront to advertise the work of the project; entry was by pressing a buzzer and then there was a narrow flight of stairs to climb. It didn't encourage contact with local people. It was not until earlier this year (1994) that the John Reynolds Centre, a new community-centre-cum-project-HQ, jointly funded by NCH Action For Children, South Glamorgan County Council and Cardiff City Council, was opened. It has a café, a shop selling secondhand toys, baby clothes and equipment, a toy library, a hall, and a launderette—there's not one on the estate, and the project's washing machine in the old premises was much in demand. The local job shop is open there two days a week and a credit union has its office there.

Eventually, the intention is that this £750,000 building and the project will move from NCH Action For Children's hands into the control of local people through LLARTA—the Lower Llanrumney Area Residents and Tenants Association. This is a bold move and one already pioneered by the agency in Glasgow. There NCH Action For Children founded a community project on the giant Easterhouse Estate, and eventually withdrew to leave control in the hands of a resident-run committee.

It isn't that local people aren't able to take on the job already: but there are large numbers of practical problems and priorities within the project still to be decided. Residents have shown their interest in running their own show: the crèche, the longest-established part of the project, is run by a local woman, assisted by local women, and it was local women who were employed on the playscheme during the school summer holidays.

Because of the project's emphasis on working with younger children, it is women who have tended to be the main focus of the project's work. And as their interest has been attracted, so more of the project's work has been tailored to meet their needs as women, with special groups being set up. There is even a young mother's exchange with Stuttgart and a women's baseball team.

All this work—encouraging local people to take over responsibility from workers and the emphasis on women's issues—is underpinned by two of the project's principles: a commitment to an anti-sexist (as well as an anti-racist) approach and working in ways which empower local people.

There are, of course, problems to be met with both. But it is Nigel Billingham's hope that when LLARTA takes over the project it will be local people who will be employed to run the project, not professional workers, like himself. This is the ultimate fulfilment, perhaps, of the community work ideal.

There is nothing fanciful about this. Three local people are on full-time youth and community work courses and three more have joined to do community work part time, while a number have gone through the year-long Pre-School Playgroups Association course. Two are thinking about applying to take a social work qualifying course.

Of course, practical considerations, the struggle with daily life—'If you are a single parent, with two kids on benefit, that's job enough'—can militate against involvement by individuals. And there is the possibility that women who break away from stereotypical roles of wife, mother and homemaker, and gain insights into their full potential by running a project or sitting on a committee, may meet male opposition.

There is a danger too that the concentration on child care, and the attraction of women to the project, can mean that men see the project as 'women's work'. But the project hopes it can broaden the base of the people with whom it works. This can be slow work. Informal contacts may lead to other things in the future. For example, in the summer of 1992, a free photographic show was set up—families and individuals could come and have their photographs taken. They came once for the session and again to collect their pictures. It was a way of making contact and making the project known.

Men do, however, make a lot of use of the advice worker. Early queries were about school suspension, benefits and housing. Now demand is so great that an appointments system has had to be introduced. The worker is there three days each week and on one afternoon a solicitor is on hand to offer free legal advice. Men are also found among those who use the support group set up for people with mental health problems, like anxiety or depression. This meets for mutual support and to arrange social activities.

The project also gives space to the local health clinic once a week while the credit union (a separate NCH Action For Children project) is housed in its building. A credit union is a savings and loans co-operative (there is no commercial bank on the estate) run by volunteers (who undertake financial training before they are able to set up a union) on estates and in workplaces. Unions allow savings of as little as people can make and offer outstandingly low rates of interest on loans—about one per cent a month. They are a sort of controllable credit, encourage thrift and offer assistance with money management. They can be critical for poorer people for whom bad debts (often to money-lenders who charge rates far above those charged by commercial banks) are often the source of financial pressure which contributes to family breakdown, domestic violence and even suicide.

Supporting families, be they with two parents or one, is at the core of Llanrumney's varied work, whether it is through its low-rent caravan in Porthcawl, for people for whom a holiday is otherwise a dream, or the after-school clubs it runs. It can also allow a project worker to attend a social security tribunal with a resident. The project is working closely with Pursuit of Valued Lives—a local social services venture which aims to find community-based alternatives to dated adult training centres for people with learning difficulties, of whom a higher than average number live on the estate. A full-time worker, paid for by the local social services department, who works with everyone living in Llanrumney, is part of the project team.

Behind the serried rows of Llanrumney's front doors, along the streets where litter drifts in the wind, more goes on than the casual visitor would ever see. The project faces its problems with an unblinking eye. It has come a long way from the hut in the school playground. It knows that modest ambitions are more likely to be realized than great, but unrealistic, expectations.

MANCHESTER

The Greater Manchester Mediation Service

When Gary and Marie decided to end their marriage, it was their solicitors who got in touch with the mediation service. Against Gary's will, the couple had recently started to live apart. They argued every time they met, often in front of their children, Claire and Matthew, when Gary came to collect them. They were both very angry and needed to clear the air between them with some straight talking, before they could even start thinking of the children's needs.

Marie felt her husband was using his contact with the children to spy on her. He agreed there was some truth in this—he couldn't see the children without asking Marie to come back with him. But, through mediation, he came to understand that he needed to slacken off a little, to try to do something about the upset on the doorstep whenever he called. For a few months he arranged for his sister, who knew the children well, to collect them. Later, when he had come to accept the finality of the separation, he was able to collect them without so much pain and conflict.

Marie and Gary's marriage is just one of 152,600 that end in divorce in the UK every year, and Claire and Matthew are only two of the 150,000 children caught up in the process. The first mediation scheme began in Bristol eighteen years ago; it was an idea transplanted from North America and Australia. Today there are more than sixty such schemes. None receives government funding and many face financial difficulties that have caused some of them to close. NCH Action For Children runs the largest number of schemes in the voluntary sector and over a third of the income that funds independent mediation services is invested in its projects.

Mediation—the attempt to help separating or divorcing couples to settle their problems by agreement, without going to court—is very much in the mainstream of the organization's work. It is children who are often the victims and those most affected by divorce. Making use of the courts to settle a couple's disagreements notoriously exacerbates what is usually a very fraught, and often a painful and bitter situation: courts are adversarial, their formal procedures requiring fault to be found in the other person. All of this, leaving aside their parents' parting and the break-up of the family home, can bear very heavily on children. They can too easily find themselves caught in the middle of their parents' domestic battleground, and even become ammunition in the conflict.

The Greater Manchester Mediation Service was started in 1988. In 1993 it worked with 394 families, an increase of a quarter on the previous year. It works closely with solicitors, citizens advice bureaux, social workers, and Relate, the marriage guidance agency (especially in the 'grey' areas where couples are uncertain of the future of their relationship).

Sheena Adam, co-ordinator at the service's headquarters in Bury, has seen the service go from a situation where it was little known to one where the demands upon it are reaching saturation point. Now she and the part-time deputy co-ordinator, Louise Horne, have occasionally to put aside their development and management work, and assist the fourteen sessional workers. The service tries to ensure that no one waits more than two weeks to be seen, unlike the several months it can take for an appointment with Relate.

There is currently debate about whether attempts at mediation should be mandatory. The mediation service offered by the divorce court welfare service for problems referred to it by the court is limited, and often comes too late in the break to achieve the best results. Partly in recognition of this, some mediation services, such as that in Greater Manchester, receive some partnership funding from the court welfare service and some referrals from the court. (The probation service meets 40 per cent of the Manchester service's budget.) Only Scotland has so far even tried actively to encourage mediation. There couples are required by the courts to make an appointment with a mediation service in order to be given information about it. This at least offers those who might not have considered using the service the chance to do so.

In Manchester nearly a quarter (25 per cent) of couples using the service have been referred by solicitors, a third (30 per cent) are self-referrals, 30 per cent come from the courts, and the rest as a result of friends, relatives or other professionals referring them. Referrals from the courts are now an increasingly significant part of the total.

Most of the problems (58 per cent) with which Manchester deals involve contact (or what used to be called access), while a fifth (20 per cent) are about residence (the new term, under the Children Act 1989, replacing custody). 6 per cent of cases are about children's behaviour and their reactions to divorce. Mediation can help parents reflect on how their bitterness and anger may be affecting, or could affect, their children. It can help them explain to their children what is happening: children who are kept in the dark can feel themselves in some way to blame for what is happening. Step-family problems, which make up 4 per cent of Manchester's cases, are something else which mediation can be used to resolve.

But does it work? The figures from the Bury headquarters show that in sixty per cent of cases, full (25 per cent) or partial (35 per cent) agreement was reached. All parents leave the service with a better understanding of their children's needs and the need for co-operation, even if, at that point, they are unable to reach any agreement. This is borne out by the first study of comprehensive mediation to be published.[1] It looked at the effect of the service on finances and property, as well as children. The three-year research considered 102 couples in five projects—Bristol, Cambridge, Coventry, Northumberland and Tyneside, and Sussex. Eight out of ten couples reached agreement on at least some of the issues and four out of ten reached a complete settlement. Six out of ten felt mediation had reduced their legal bills and only two couples ended up paying more.

Sheena Adam says: 'We often have parents saying to us: "We wish we'd come earlier," and that if they hadn't come they'd not have been able to make an agreement about seeing the children at Christmas or about the buying of joint birthday presents.' Small matters maybe, but just the kind to make worse the wounds in a broken relationship.

Those who come to the service—and they can receive mediation at a number of offices borrowed or rented throughout Greater Manchester—will be seen about three times. The parents first, either together or separately, and then, if it is their wish, the children, with or without their parents. It is the clients who set the pace. Some negotiate agreements and return a year later to review them; others agree matters for a six-month period and then come back to talk about the next six months.

'We are trying to avoid being seen as a quick fix,' says Sheena Adam, 'with us being seen as people who say: "Here's the agreement—now get on with it yourselves." But neither, on the other hand, do we want to be a permanent referee in people's lives, so that they become too dependent on us. If they don't want us any more—and it's up to them to say—they can cope. We are here to make ourselves redundant for them.

'Of course, we know that human beings are not super-rational creatures, otherwise they wouldn't need us or the courts. We are trying to help people express their hurt and their anger in order to get rid of them. We don't want them to repress these feelings because then we have the pressure cooker syndrome and everybody is ready to explode. We have found that people's period of adjustment to a split varies greatly. Six years later there are still some people who feel the hurt.'

Is the hurt assuaged if they have found a new relationship? It depends as to whether the new relationship is what Sheena Adam calls 'a defensive alliance', a relationship formed to protect the 'hurt' party, or whether it is a genuine relationship. The first sort has within it the seeds of potential failure.

The reasons for separations differ. Some people marry young to escape their home environment, an escape which they then find imprisons them. Those who come to the Bury office are no different from the general run of separating and divorcing couples: their reasons range from just 'growing apart' to 'he threw me down the stairs.'[2]

One woman said: 'We were married young, and we were married for a long time. I was unhappy and I thought that Dan was unhappy, too. Eventually I took action. I felt all the guilt and blame and resented it enormously. I was the one who articulated the concern, though it was equally true for Dan, he has since said that. I felt we could have more fulfilling lives if we separated and that we could parent the children, too.'[3]

The eventual separation and divorce may, indeed, be best for the children but it can, all the same, be painful and confusing. Thus, Manchester has now established a counselling service for children. One room in the offices has been converted to a children's room with brightly painted walls and toys and books, some of which are used to help the children express their feelings.

The youngest child seen was eight but most are younger teenagers. How children react to divorce differs from child to child, age to age. For those in the pre-school years fear, fantasy, bewilderment, denial and the inhibition of aggression against the parent with whom they live while showing it against the other may be among the ways they react. Those aged six to eight can show grief, a 'pervading sadness' and feelings of deprivation, yearning, anger with their mother, the suppression of anger against their father.

It is thirteen- to eighteen-year-olds who may worry about sex and marriage, who may mourn, show anger, display conflicting loyalties toward their parents, exhibit greater maturity and 'moral growth', have a changed part to play in their family. They may have a more realistic view of the financial implications of their parents' breakup, but also fail to cope and show some loss of external values and controls.[4] Children of any age may find themselves moving from what they have seen as a safe world to one which, if it does not appear unsafe is, at least, uncertain.

While the service is confidential for parents as well as children, Manchester (unlike some services) will not see children without their parents' knowledge. The service is about helping a family function better; to see children without their parents' knowledge may appear to parents to set some family members against others. But the Manchester service is also part of a wider network of NCH Action For Children services—from family centres to residential units and helplines—and children may be referred to these when it is felt appropriate.

Often conflict is ended by the fact of divorce itself, and a certain stability may be attained when domestic strife is formally ended. But for children, uncertain and groping to understand a situation which is not of their making but has been forced upon them, mediation may be the best hope when reconciliation is no longer possible.

OXFORDSHIRE

Penhurst Special School

Emma is eleven years old, partially-sighted, cannot move without the aid of her wheelchair, and has a vocabulary of not much more than thirty words. In the corridor by her brightly decorated room, with its pictures and mobiles hanging over her bed and music centre, there are posters about Montezuma, the Aztec king, and the thirteenth-century explorer Marco Polo. The visitor wonders what these can mean to Emma, whose real joy is to lie on the vibrating bed and operate it by moving her head on and off the control panel. The answer is that no one can be sure.

Neither can anyone be sure what the Cadbury Centre, the Midland's theme park tribute to the chocolate-making industry, meant to Emma when she visited it. But what David Southeard, head teacher of Penhurst Special School, Oxfordshire, is sure of is that if he or his staff based their work with Emma on a response to what she and his other pupils may *appear* to need, they might offer them very little.

The staff at Penhurst develop individually tailored programmes to meet the needs of their children, whatever the stage of their physical and intellectual development. They also work on the assumption that some things in the lives of children who have profound physical and mental disabilities are not measurable, and not open to objective evaluation— such as the ability to read, or to move one's limbs.

In 1904, when the Home turned a mill-owner's two large, late Victorian, semi-detached houses into a children's home, it provided teaching in the basement to those physically disabled children unable to attend local schools. Today, the buildings have spread over the once spacious grounds. But, just as the staff of 1904 believed even disabled children to be educable, at a time when society had its doubts, so today Penhurst staff believe that disabilities of any kind should not close the door on opportunities, experiences and formal education for any of those who attend the school.

The pupils at Penhurst are placed in classes according to their chronological age, the type of curriculum they need to follow and their level of maturity. Whatever their developmental age, pupils do, by varying degrees, move forward. Some of the children are part of the school's Motor Education Programme. This makes use of some aspects of conductive education, imported from Hungary, which is now sufficiently accepted in Britain to receive government funding. It remains, however, available at only a few centres.

The school's programme is one of physical stimulation, consistent language, rhythm and repetition to make a child aware of itself, so that he or she is enabled to learn how to control movements and positions. Tasks may be as simple (to the non-disabled, at least) as sitting up straight with both feet flat. The child is encouraged, by example, to see how certain moves can give greater freedom: he or she may hold onto a handbar and so learn balance and how to sit. This may lead, as balance improves, to letting go of the bar with one hand, in order to use the free hand for other tasks. Motor education is much more than physiotherapy—it is about learning how to balance, move and communicate.

Emma is one of fifteen termly boarders. Eleven children live at the school during the week, two attend as day pupils and one girl lives there throughout the year. All have a physical disability—no child is able to walk unaided—and half of the pupils have a profound learning difficulty. All, in varying degrees, have contact with their parents. 'Although we are a residential school I always emphasize that what remains most important for our pupils is their families and life outside,' says David Southeard.

With modern facilities of the highest standards—a hydrotherapy pool, sixteen computers for teaching, and various kinds of other advanced equipment—and seventy-five staff, the annual fees for termly boarders of £40,000 dwarf those of the top public schools, Eton and Roedean. Children more and more come to the school on the initiative of their parents—they undergo a three-day assessment before being accepted——but parents make no contribution to fees, which are met mostly by local education authorities, sometimes by LEAs and social services departments together, and, occasionally, by health authorities.

While there are other residential special schools for children with the most severe disabilities, run by local authorities and voluntary bodies, this is the only one run by NCH Action For Children (it has three other residential special schools catering for children with other kinds of special needs). Penhurst takes children from the age of five to nineteen, but David Southeard says he would be disappointed if a child came at five and was still with him at nineteen. Children need to come and go, according to their needs and developmental stage.

More parents are now seeking entry for their children younger than five because of the profundity of their disability; and more parents are asking that their children be accepted in their mid-teens because they themselves are getting older and the children too difficult for them to manage. There is no child too disabled for the school to accept. However, children with very challenging behaviour are not accepted as they could put at risk the very vulnerable children for whom it cares.

The children live in groups of eight—some have their own rooms, most share with another—with six residential social workers for each group in single storey buildings. The residential staff cater for the children's non-education needs: social, personal and domestic. Education is carried out by trained teaching staff, assisted by teaching assistants and volunteers. Medical staff are also on hand. It is a characteristic of the modern ways of working with such children that Penhurst's physiotherapists and speech therapist, though they have their own offices, are more likely to be where the children are—in the classrooms, or in their rooms—than remove them to some 'special' place for speech or physiotherapy.

The trend today is for children with both mental and physical dis-abilities to be taught in mainstream schools. But none of the Penhurst children is at a developmental stage which would make that a practical possibility. Penhurst does offer the National Curriculum, which is modi-fied to meet each child's abilities. After entry assessment, individual learning objectives are drawn up for each child to ensure a teaching and learning programme tailored to his or her needs. In class, they follow their own programmes and learn at their own rate. A variety of communication methods are used from the relatively sophisticated Bliss to the more basic Rebus (both picture symbol methods), as well as eye-pointing (where pupils indicate wishes by looking at words on cards) to voice output electronic communication aids.

High staff ratios ensure an atmosphere of busyness and activity but, as Linda Sinfield, a teacher, says all children need time to play on their own, to enjoy their own company. For two children, with different degrees of disability, this takes different forms. Carole lies on the vibrating bed, operating it herself. Her pleasures are sensory. Gary plays with a toy shop: he understands the idea of shops and shopping and although he cannot speak, whenever anyone passes him he makes a noise which says: 'Come into my shop,' and each 'customer' does.

While respecting the need for peace, quiet and personal space, the school environment is also stimulating. In the rest rooms there are ball pools, vibrating beds, mobiles and optikinetic projectors which throw swirling colours on the walls and ceilings. Penhurst believes in a holistic approach to the children: they are more than the sum of their parts, more than receivers of knowledge or recipients of experience. While the school is not denominational, it has regular Christian assemblies and offers religious teaching. However, alternative arrangements can be made for children of other faiths or those whose parents do not wish them to take part in religious observance or to receive such teaching. Emphasis is also placed on personal and social education, learning to live with others and enjoy their company. This is especially important for children whose past relationships will often have been with adults only, rather than other children.

Teaching at schools like Penhurst is not easy, admits David Southeard. 'But,' he says, 'special education is about helping to enable children to exert whatever control they have at their disposal, no matter how limited it may be in our opinion, over the world in which they live. It is about being involved in choices and decisions that affect them, even if they are as basic as whether they are to wear red socks or blue socks, or what breakfast cereal to eat or asking someone to do something for them. We aren't talking about independence as you and I may understand it and enjoy it but it is about independence all the same—having opinions, making choices, being able to say "I want this" or "I don't like that."'

With residential care often regarded (even in social services) as the last resort rather than a positive choice, does Penhurst feel itself in any way outside the mainstream of practice and thinking? David Southeard has no doubts at all. The children here could not take part in mainstream education as it is currently organized, and he feels that the work and philosophy of the school reflects what is new and innovative in education and social work: it uses the National Curriculum; it is alive to the increasing role that parents want to play. But he recognizes that any residential establishment is in danger of being inward-looking and separated from the mainstream of the life about it.

And so Penhurst puts great emphasis not only on bringing local people and others into the school as much as possible (there are regular information days, and local pregnant women use the hydrotherapy pool for aquanatal classes) but also in getting the children out as much as possible. It makes use of the facilities of Chipping Norton, the little Cotswold market town where it is situated; it recruits volunteers through the town's volunteer bureau; it takes its children to plays and concerts in the local community, just as it invites local school children to participate at events at Penhurst; and one morning a week different groups of its pupils attend a local primary school.

David Southeard himself is often out and about talking to local groups, sometimes unsettling their misconceptions about children with disabilities; a necessary job, he says, if Penhurst's work is also to educate the public. When the information days are held, those who attend are taken around but never see any children. At first it seems strange that they should see the hi-tech equipment, the well-equipped classrooms, the displays of achievement, the cheery bedrooms and all else that makes Penhurst, without sight of those for whom it exists. But, at the end of the tour he does not need to give the answer why on that day the children have been invisible. The reason goes to the heart of Penhurst's philosophy. They are not exhibits. And, as David Southeard says: 'We treat our children with respect and dignity and help them to come to an appreciation of their own importance and value.'

The names of the children have been changed.

SOUTH GLAMORGAN

The South Glamorgan Options Project

'Options' says it all. The Options Project began in 1984 believing that parents of children with learning difficulties wanted practical support for themselves—someone to do the shopping occasionally, or to take their child for a hospital appointment if they couldn't—but when the parents themselves were asked what they wanted, their priorities were different. They wanted support for their children. And so, although Options does offer a sitting service to care for the children when parents go out, its main thrust is to give children and young people with learning difficulties—from toddlers to young adults—the support they need to take part in leisure activities and play schemes.

That switch in understanding and the change to offering what consumers of services want, rather than what professionals think they want, is now the way of the welfare world. Options can take some credit for anticipating, even in its comparatively short life, much current prescription: it is important to listen to those using services and not to think that professionals know best.

The project works with an average of sixty children and young people in a county where there are estimated to be 360 children and young people, aged nought to nineteen, with a learning difficulty. None of what it does could be achieved without volunteers. Options has a project leader, four half-time workers, a secretary, and two employment trainees (from the government scheme to give unemployed people a year's experience of work different from what they have done). But it is the volunteers (there were ninety-seven in 1991–92 who worked with eighty-four youngsters) who are the backbone of its work.

Most volunteers are recruited informally—someone has a friend or partner who has volunteered—or by personal canvassing by Options' staff. The summer play scheme work has been undertaken largely by young people aged 16–21, recruited by visits to schools and higher and further education establishments. There is also some recruitment of volunteers (as opposed to employment trainees) through job centres. The recession has given an unusual twist to volunteering: increasingly men are coming forward, many of whom have formerly worked in male-dominated industries like the mines or steel. It's also a pattern that has influenced the employment trainees: in 1992 there were three, two of whom were men; in 1993 there were again three, all of whom were men.

Options has more volunteers than it can cope with. Partly, this is due to the staff resources which would be needed to make use of all of them. But, also, the county spreads itself along the south Wales coast and northward to the valleys, and is of a size that the ideal match of volunteer to child or young person may be frustrated by the distance they live from each other or by problems of transport.

Volunteers, who are subject to police checks, undergo training to acquaint them with Options' work: how statutory and voluntary services operate; what 'learning difficulties' means; attitudes and popular images of learning difficulties; as well as practical matters like who will support them and how to claim expenses. This training is compulsory but there is another (voluntary) tier. Here volunteers can be taught basic signing and first aid, or learn about sexuality, autism, epilepsy, communication and feeding, and child protection. Just as Options' services reflect users' needs, so its training is geared to what volunteers say they need to know.

What lies behind the phrase about supporting children and young people to give them the 'opportunity to access and enjoy local amenities and participate in the local community', as the Options' literature puts it? It is teaming them up with a volunteer so that, for example, they can attend a club, Cub or Scout troop, go to the cinema, use public transport, follow a hobby like snooker or pottery, go riding or play football; or, by working alongside the volunteer, develop skills. The play scheme allows children to attend accompanied by a volunteer, while Saturday clubs allow youngsters the chance to take part in play and other activities with those of their own age and to give parents and carers a break.

All these facilities are integrated: the child or young person attends with children who do not have disabilities, and an incidental aspect of this is that those youngsters are made aware of what disability means and what disabled youngsters (and older people) require to live ordinary lives. Options has also been specific about raising of awareness: in 1988 it won an award from the weekly social services magazine *Community Care* to fund a teaching pack for children in two Cardiff junior schools to teach them about learning difficulties.

Even today, with the old long-stay hospitals closing, children with learning difficulties living with their families and many more people with a learning difficulty living in the community, the importance of such an initiative can't be underestimated. Brigitte Gater, project leader, points out that whenever a scheme is proposed whereby people with a learning difficulty will be resettled from hospital care in an ordinary residential street, there are public protests. There's an ambivalence here, as she also points out: it is the neighbours who are the first to come round with a cup of tea once the residents have moved in.

Certainly, parents of children with learning difficulties too often experience isolation. Not for nothing was a survey of leisure needs on Cardiff's large, suburban Llanrumney estate, entitled *Confined in the Community*.[1] What went for the parents in Llanrumney, where there is a higher than average proportion of youngsters with a learning difficulty, can safely be said to prevail elsewhere, not only in South Glamorgan but throughout the UK. The survey found that enjoyment of activities was hampered by lack of information, lack of support and lack of money. A club might boast that it was open to everyone, but if a parent had no way of getting his or her child to it, the child was effectively debarred. (Likewise, if a youngster exhibits challenging behaviour—if he or she acts disruptively—and there's no support offered, that group which proclaims that it welcomes everyone, says in effect: 'Sorry, we can't have you.')

Caz Whitfield is a parent whose ten-year-old daughter Tracey, diagnosed at three as having an autistic tendency, has benefited from Options' work. When she was a week old Tracey started having infantile spasms and it took Caz and Paul Whitfield a year to convince the doctors that something was wrong. They diagnosed epilepsy. The family received no help before the diagnosis, but it was a specialist health visitor who detailed what support might be available and mentioned Options. Tracy joined a summer play scheme that her older sister could also attend; then Options provided a volunteer sitter, and when Tracey joined a Saturday club (to which her mother takes her, alternating week by week with a volunteer), her sister went, too. The Whitfields are also part of Barnardo's' Family Link scheme, where they are paired with a family with whom Tracey stays one night a week and occasionally at weekends.

For Caz and Paul Whitfield, Options' services offer them not only occasional relief but also allow Tracey the routine and stimulation which a child with autism needs: school holidays with its disruption to routine can often cause such children to get bored and can make them disruptive. One result has been, her mother says, that Tracey's concentration has improved: she can now watch a video. Today she attends a Saturday Club; in future years Options may help her attend a youth club in the evening.

Leisure is important for everyone, but for families who say they are 'isolated' and 'confined', it can never be a luxury. As the report mentioned above stated: 'It is very important that leisure is recognized as a major component of respite care for families who have a child or young adult with special needs.'

In some ways, too, segregated facilities fuel that sense of isolation that parents and their children feel—a child may be collected each day by taxi for a twelve-mile journey to a special school, while children in the same street walk to the local school. A child may have no local friends but may know lots of other children with learning difficulties who live in the four corners of the county.

Options does not want to spread its wings too far. It will not, for example, offer volunteers to support children in mainstream schools. Partly because its remit is leisure activities and play schemes, but also because if a school cannot offer the support which a child with a disability may need to be in the mainstream, then Options does not see its role as being to plug gaps in local authority provision.

From its earliest days, Options has responded to the needs which parents said they (or their children) had. Now it aims to bring users of its services to the centre of what it does and how it works. It has set up an advisory project committee. Membership includes two members of South Glamorgan social services department (one of whom has the remit to work with people from ethnic minorities), a local Methodist minister, two parents, two volunteers, and two teenage users, who attend with their volunteers, there to help them, if need be. It also wants to recruit two young people of primary school age. They would probably not be able to attend; the committee meets in the evening so that parents can attend, and there is also the question whether children on committees may be overawed by being outnumbered by adults. But the intention would be for them to have an adult representative to voice their views.

In the field of working with families who have a child with a learning difficulty, there is often the dilemma of knowing who is the user—the child or the parent. Sometimes this can cause a clash of interests. Occasionally, the views of parents may not accord with the philosophy underpinning the project. For example, one parent asked why Options didn't organize group outings for children. The project doesn't want to be running 'visits for the handicapped' and have, say, forty youngsters arriving by the vanload at somewhere like Alton Towers.

Brigitte Gater recognizes the dilemma. Sometimes, she says, parents accept the principles of 'normalization'—the idea that people with a disability should be enabled to live as ordinary a life as possible in the community—but when it comes to their own child they may say: 'Yes, it's OK for Susan over there, but not for my child.' There is no easy answer to this. Options offers services to help children and young people take part in integrated activities; it does not force them on parents, but, equally, it won't place children in segregated clubs or bus a dozen of them off on a trip.

The key to Options' work is flexibility. It hopes to receive additional funding from the local authority to offer holiday support for twenty children. This scheme will let children and young people with a learning difficulty and their families choose from a range of support services, so they can have holidays and short breaks tailor-made to their needs. In planning the holiday they will be helped by Options staff, who will make the necessary practical arrangements and link the families to paid workers and volunteers.

Options is a project which is about working in the community. Its pitch is not to have people come to its small office, behind terraced houses two miles from Cardiff's city centre, but to go out to meet them, to reach out to *all* groups. Cardiff, especially, is a mixed community—there are Somalis, both long-settled and refugees, Chinese, Hindus and Bengalis, in the same streets as people who speak Welsh in the pub as much as at home. Options is acutely aware that it has far to go in meeting the needs of families from ethnic minority backgrounds.

Now Options wants to appoint a black worker. The aim is not only to have a worker to relate one-to-one with families from black and ethnic minority communities, who anyway will be as different one from another as from the majority community. It is also to have a team-member who can broaden the knowledge and skills of the Options team to help them to work more effectively with families from ethnic minority backgrounds. The presence of a black worker would more accurately reflect the *whole* community in which Options works.

STRATHCLYDE

The Children and Families Counselling Project

In the early days it was 'the battered baby syndrome', the discovery—or, more accurately, the naming—of child abuse, the age-old social problem which Stephenson would have recognized. When Dr Henry Kempe and his colleagues drew attention to it in 1962 [1] they could never have predicted how in a quarter of a century new and other forms of abuse would pile one on top of the other: physical abuse, emotional abuse, neglect, sexual abuse, and, then, the elaborations of so-called satanic and ritual abuse.

And in those twenty-five years the subject was never long out of the headlines. The 'scandals' cast a shadow across social services and their care of children. There was the long and tragic procession of child abuse inquiries in the wake of the deaths of children, beginning with Maria Colwell in 1974 [2]. Later, the scandals took on a new aspect as whole local authority departments—Cleveland, Orkneys, Rochdale—as well as individual social workers were seen to be at fault.

Media sound and fury and the public concern about the often horrifying deaths, injuries and abuse which children suffer can too easily cause the quiet work which goes on behind a handsome Georgian terrace house in Glasgow to be overlooked. The Children and Families Counselling Project is neighbour to banks and architects' offices, a few minutes from Glasgow's city centre. It opened in 1990 as a pilot, was followed by ten more, and by the time NCH Action For Children launched a £4 million appeal for a national network of treatment centres in September 1992, five more were in the planning stage.

Several hundred victims and their families have in that time passed through the anonymous door in Glasgow—it announces only that it is an office of NCH Action For Children on the nameplate. Yet the project is modest enough. It does not even occupy all the building. There are two project workers and a project leader—two of them social workers, one a counsellor—and an administrative worker.

The idea of the treatment centres grew out of concerns which gradually emerged from other NCH Action For Children work. A number of projects—residential, the Careline telephone counselling service and some family centres—began to mention 'child sexual abuse'. Discussion revealed an area of difficulty: more children were disclosing that they had been abused in this way; local authorities were responding more effectively in terms of disclosure; there was better co-operation with the police, health services and housing authorities—but there was not much help available for the children unless they happened to fit into the areas where help was already being provided, such as an ordinary children's home or some kind of day care.

NCH Action For Children's fears that there was little assistance available to sexually abused children and their families were confirmed when it carried out a survey of treatment facilities on behalf of the Department of Health.[3] There were 60,592 children on local authority at-risk registers, of whom 5,950 had been, or were in danger of being, sexually abused. But there were only eight projects focusing specifically on sexual abuse in the whole of England and Wales (the survey excluded Scotland, for which the Department of Health is not responsible). There were another 182 facilities which did some kind of work with sexually abused children, but for most this was a minor part of their activities. Around half the local authorities had no treatment facilities, and what there was tended to be clustered about large urban areas, such as London, Birmingham, Leeds, Sheffield and Manchester.

NCH Action For Children's first reaction was to campaign for services to be developed. As Tom White, principal and chief executive, explains: 'The plan was to use our resources to encourage other agencies to work and ensure that work was on a multi-disciplinary basis so that it was not just local authorities: health authorities, probation service, and, if we could get them, other organizations as well (we do run a number of projects in which the NSPCC is involved).'

When this did not bear fruit—although it was acknowledged that such services were needed—it decided to take on the job itself. If the organization could be of use to adolescent and adult survivors of sexual abuse, it might also offer a service to those whose history of abuse was more recent.

And so, the Children and Families Counselling Project came into being. The service is specifically tailored to meet the counselling needs of children who have been sexually abused (who will also have suffered emotionally) and their families. Some children may also have been physically abused.

Prevention rather than simply protection is a key issue but the tight financial girdles which encase local authorities have forced many of them to concentrate their efforts on the initial stages of investigation of child abuse and immediate protection, with subsequent counselling and therapy being something of a luxury which increasingly can be ill afforded.

The Glasgow centre and the network of projects built upon it was pioneering because it offers counselling for the whole family—since abuse is not a problem for the victim alone, but one which affects the parents and brothers and sisters. However, the centre will not counsel parents who are abusers. This is partly for legal reasons—the possibility that there may be an inadvertent interfering with the evidence; but also because counselling an abuser who is a family member—often the father—would take additional time, energy and approaches beyond the project's resources. In Scotland work with abusers was undertaken by the Royal Scottish Society for the Prevention of Cruelty to Children's Overnewton Centre (now closed), where, however, staff ratios of one worker to one abuser severely limited the number of perpetrators who could be seen.[4]

Those who use the Glasgow centre's services are usually seen for six months, with one hourly session a week. By the end of this intensive therapy it is hoped that the stain of abuse will no longer dominate or damage children's and family's lives so much. Even if it never wipes away what has happened, therapy should leave the child and family more settled and secure. For the project workers this is painful work, which provokes intense feelings. After two or three years many feel the need to move on to other kinds of social work.

If sexual abuse brings pain to the victims, their families and those who work with them, it also provokes ambivalence in society. At work here are factors such as society's incredulity that such things can be done to children; an inability to see the family other than as the positive, nurturing force it is popularly imagined to be; and even the fact that sexual abuse of children touches upon difficult and painful parts of some people's sexual makeup.

Cleveland County Council, whatever the shortcomings of its own practice evident in the Butler-Sloss report,[5] was not thanked for uncover-ing a nasty side to family life within its borders. Child abuse work has also been bedevilled by the lack of generally accepted figures—the problems of separating incidence from the reporting of abuse—but it may be that ten per cent of adults have at one time been abused. In Scotland there are 3,513 children on child protection registers. Strathclyde, which the project serves (it can only offer a consultancy service to other NCH Action For Children projects elsewhere in the country) has between 800 to 900 of them, of whom 230 are thought to have been sexual abused.[6]

The Glasgow project gives evidence of the cycle of abuse: some of those who have themselves been abused as children may, in turn, become abusers. It has also seen children from residential care who have been abused by other children in care, who have themselves been abused.

Like other NCH Action For Children projects, the Glasgow centre works closely with the local authority, in this case Strathclyde social work department. The department refers children and families to the centre, although some make their own contact. Financially, Strathclyde is now the largest partner. It was the Scottish Office which provided £50,000 a year for three years, when the project began, with NCH Action For Children putting in £70,000 a year for the same period. The council gave nothing in the first year, £3,000 in the second and £5,000 in the third year. Today it meets 75 per cent of the costs.

The pressure on the service, with need outstripping what it is able to offer, means, perhaps, that it cannot serve everyone who gets in touch. Instead it takes only the more difficult cases.

Sexual abuse respects no barriers. It is as likely to happen among the tree-lined suburban avenues of, say, Bearsden as it is on the large and deprived Easterhouse estate. What, then, are its causes? It is about the exercise of power within the family, even where, as in about 10 per cent of cases, the abuser is a woman.

The project's child-centred approach focuses on empowering children, encouraging them to make choices. The child-centred focus means that project workers will work on how the child perceives the problem. For example, the adult may see the main issues as the trauma of sexual assault; the child may see it as the break-up of the family, or problems at school. Counselling is about allowing children to under-stand what has happened to them; to understand their feelings; to remove any feelings of guilt they may feel; to rebuild self-respect when they may have felt soiled, and to restore their trust in others. The project has two brightly-decorated and well- but simply furnished rooms for counselling. Here there are toys, which can often allow the children to express feelings, as can games. The atmosphere encourages the expression of feeling. Helping people relax is important. One child may be withdrawn, another may be aggressive, demonstrating this either towards others or towards him- or herself by, for example, head banging.

Sometimes the work needs to go further than the counselling room. Apart from the referrals to rape crisis centres or women's refuges for older victims, centre staff will sometimes, with the child's knowledge, speak to teachers when what has happened to their pupils is causing problem behaviour. Because abuse is carried out in secret it is important that children know that workers are in touch with the school, that 'secrets' are not being kept from them. On occasion the project has offered training for teachers in a school with which it works closely.

Social work's successes are notoriously difficult to measure, and this is particularly so in the field of abuse. Who is to say how well trust has been rebuilt? Who can discover—even predict—what the eight-year-old will be like as a forty-year-old? The University of Glasgow has completed a study based on the centre's work[7] and NCH Action For Children has joined nationally with Guy's Hospital, London, for study following children over two years to look at the effectiveness of treatment methods.[8]

The headlines which occasionally erupt on the front pages of newspapers and the publicity of the often sensational trials of abusers can easily obscure the private pain of those who have been abused, the tragedies within families, and the slow and patient work of places such as the centre.

SUFFOLK

The West Suffolk Youth Justice Centre

By the time David (not his real name) was fifteen he had been before the courts eight times for burglary. Cautions, discharges, and a twenty-four-hour spell in an attendance centre seemed to offer no obstacles to a fast-approaching career in the penal system. Today, with emphasis on 'getting tough' with young offenders, running up a string of offences like that would almost certainly land him with a spell in youth custody. But, three years ago, his last sentence did not see a door shut behind him but rather one open, when the court made a Specified Activities Supervision Order, to be overseen by the West Suffolk Youth Justice Centre.

The order laid down a number of activities David would undertake, which included some kind of reparation work in the community (other youngsters coming to the centre have cleared churchyards and worked in parks, elderly people's homes and adult training centres for people with learning difficulties). The order also asked David to ask himself why he did what he did. He had never thought about it before. For young offenders, confronting what they have done and asking themselves why they did it can be one of the hardest things, a difficulty that a stream of self-justification cannot overcome or disguise.

Three times a week for a year, David had to meet one of the centre's three youth justice social workers. He would not only have to look at the consequences of his offences both for himself and his victims. He would also look at events which might have led up to it, and at the reasons for his subsequent behaviour. His regime was one young offenders at the centre are commonly put through. They may be asked to select the kind of excuses which they would use if committing an offence—'it was an accident'; 'it was others who did the job, I just hung about outside'; or 'most people are insured against theft, they don't care', and so on. They are also asked to study a diagram which has boxes leading off from the offence which are headed: 'Where?', 'Why?', 'When?', 'Who?' and 'What?'

At the same time, young offenders may also be asked to look at what they enjoy doing, where and how they do it, whether they do it with others, and how often it is done, and complete a form to assist the analysis. Hypothetical situations in which they could find themselves are also analysed. Someone is talking about a friend behind their back: how could they be tackled about it? A friend borrows a record that is returned scratched: what can be done about it? Another part of the programme looks at objectives and how they can be achieved. These can include being better able to control feelings; stopping smoking; feeling more relaxed; managing depression; resisting pressure from others; being less reserved in company; being more energetic; or finding ways of occupying time.

The work can also include, where the victim is in agreement, making a written or personal verbal apology. To meet a victim can not only make an offender remorseful but it can also temper the anger of the victim, who might gain insight and understanding when they see why the young offender did it, and their circumstances. There may perhaps be a realization that giving such young people a custodial sentence may not be the solution. The centre hopes that personal reparation schemes whereby offenders carry out some kind of work for the victim can be undertaken. But when this can't be arranged, offenders, in confronting what they have done, can be asked to put themselves in the situation of the victim. The burglar, for example, might be asked to describe coming home. What did the house look like? How did the victim feel? How would he, the offender, have felt if were his home? What would be his first reactions? What would he have done next? Meetings are also arranged with the local Victim Support workers and visits to prisons are planned.

In these attempts to explore how the offender has ended up where he has, and where life has led him, 'life snakes' are sometimes used. A drawing of a snake is marked with triangles along the length of either side of its body and into these are written 'good' and 'bad' experiences. These can often reveal other problems such as physical or sexual abuse; confusion about sexuality; or rejection by a step-parent.

David had another problem, one not uncommon in young offenders. He had stopped attending school and he was encouraged by his worker to return. Although he was eventually to leave early, he did complete his school time. Today he is a past statistic on the centre's books. His criminal record has been rolled up and he hasn't committed another offence.

The centre began in April 1992, having grown out of the West Suffolk Alternatives to Custody project, which started in 1987. Like its predecessor, the centre is a partnership between NCH Action For Children and Suffolk social services department. The local authority funds 80 per cent of the cost, with the agency picking up the rest of the bill, employing the four professional staff and offering training, and providing the modest terraced building a short distance from Bury St Edmunds' historical town centre from which the project operates. The comparatively few staff are backed up by twenty sessional workers. Uniquely, the council has contracted out all its criminal justice work to the centre and its twin, which covers the north of the county.

The centre provides a variety of programmes and services, including preparing pre-sentencing reports for the courts, acting as the independent adult legally required to be present when young people are charged with an offence, and supporting those on bail.

Confronting offending and getting youngsters to think about their lives are also included in programmes other than those ordered by the courts. The Specified Activities Supervision Order makes such programmes mandatory. The successful 'caution-plus' scheme, which includes some of the work that David went through, together with a police caution, has one disadvantage against a court order. It is not compulsory. A youngster may agree to take part after being cautioned, but can back out with impunity. But only two have done so in as many years. An analysis by the centre of its records found that 70 per cent of those who underwent 'caution-plus' for the two years from June 1991 did not reoffend. With the Home Office's own statistics now showing that 85 per cent of young men and 49 per cent of young women, aged fifteen to sixteen, who have been in youth custody, are reconvicted within two years,[1] alternatives to custody appear to make practical sense.

It has been argued in the United States, though, that even these comparisons, favourable though they are to alternatives to custody projects, are invidious:

> It is unnecessary to demonstrate, as most experimental projects appear pressured to do, that recidivism rates are lower when offenders are retained in the community. Given the fact that expensive and overcrowded institutions are not doing the job they are supposed to be doing, it is appropriate to expect that less costly, less personally damaging alternatives will be utilised whenever they are at least as effective [my emphasis] as imprisonment.[2]

But while the West Suffolk project attempts to deal with offending at a deeper level than any prison or young offenders' institution can do—and avoid the damaging effects associated with incarceration—the reoffending rates, encouraging though they are, are probably higher than they would be if the centre were dealing with the broad range of young offenders. As it is, it works with the most serious and committed offenders, that is, those in danger of receiving a custodial sentence.

The centre works with more than 200 young people aged ten to nearly eighteen each year. With the government intent on another round of policies aimed at 'getting tough with young offenders' (the politicians' shorthand for locking them up), even fewer will have the opportunity of an alternative to custody. A 'persistent' young offender will be deemed to be one who has committed three imprisonable offences. At the moment, there is no consistency to why some young people end up in custody and others get non-custodial sentences. Evidence from another NCH Action For Children project showed that there was no significant difference in the offences committed by those referred to it and those who went to prison or a young offenders' institution.[3]

But what does distinguish those youngsters who come to the West Suffolk project—and its equivalents elsewhere—is that they are in danger of receiving a custodial sentence. The aim is to keep young people out of the custodial system, and even to help keep them out of the courts. All the evidence shows that appearing in court is often a one-way street into further offending, reconviction, being locked up and graduating, in adulthood, to prison. For many, many youngsters offending is an episode in their adolescence which they can be helped to come through. That doesn't mean that they won't be punished—community options are not 'soft' alternatives. But *how* the criminal justice system treats them will be important in determining the future course of their lives.

But how does the work differ from that of local authority social workers? Social workers would be unlikely to be able to offer as intense a service as can the centre. Centre workers visit youngsters in their homes, although they also have use of premises, like probation offices, dotted about the vast rural area of west and south Suffolk which the project covers, if needed. More resources for the centre would allow preventive work, often with families. Youngsters' attendance at the centre may vary according to what is needed—a session on confronting offending behaviour may take half a day, while a morning may be spent on preparing for a job interview. Reviewing work done so far could take an hour.

The key to much of the work is for workers to get under the offender's skin, to attempt to see why he or she (unusually West Suffolk has a higher proportion of young women on its books than is found elsewhere) has committed the offence. Only by attempting to understand can there be some hope of changing behaviour.

There are all manner of reasons why offences are committed but some common threads in the lives of the youngsters can be picked out: unemployment; difficulties at school and sometimes expulsion; living in a single-parent family (usually with the mother); poverty (sixteen- to eighteen-year-olds are now denied benefit and parents will often either be on income support or in low paid jobs). Many are low achievers not through lack of innate ability, but because of their social and family circumstances. This makes many of them reluctant to go on Youth Training Schemes: they see the training element, however mistakenly, as too reminiscent of the school they rejected (or which, they may think, rejected them). Some of the young people are still at school, but of the rest about half are either in jobs (which are too often menial work in factories or jobs like strawberry picking), on YTS, or a few at college. The rest have, literally, nothing to do. Even when a job is found, it may not be possible to take it up because of poor public transport.

At one level the project can be justified on a very simple argument: does society want young offenders dealt with by being locked up for a period with the proven likelihood that they will reoffend, or does it want some real attempt made to actually change their behaviour? There's another argument—an economic one—which is perfectly suited to the government's own themes of value-for-money, effective use of resources, and economy with the public purse. A local rotary club's members, often business people, are frequently the victims of crime. Graham Harrison, centre manager, addressing them, might ask them how they would react if they had a product which didn't do the job it was made to do and cost more than another product which worked at least as well, and in some cases, better than the first product, while costing far less. A referral to the project costs about £250 a week. A week in prison sets back the taxpayer £1,900.

SUTTON COLDFIELD

Premier Way

Anyone looking for Princess Alice Drive, the great children's community, part of the National Children's Home set up as a self-sufficient estate in the 1880s, would be disappointed. The original buildings that remain are boarded up, and the land has been sold for development. Now a Tesco's store, a garage, a road and a roundabout cut through what was the middle of the estate—the great green surrounded by the houses in which the children lived.[1]

But arising, phoenix-like, from this is a project as attuned to the 1990s as was the home to its day: Premier Way now provides a quality service for children and young people with severe learning difficulties. But Premier Way's physical position is not coincidental. It opened in 1991 as a descendant of Shaftesbury House, the last remaining part of Princess Alice Drive, which, toward the end of its life, specialized in work with children with disabilities. The building which housed Shaftesbury House still stands but was unsuitable for modern practice, and so the project was reborn as Premier Way.

Premier Way consists of two purpose-built bungalows, each large enough to house six residents. At the time of writing (March 1994) they have six residents who are multiply disabled, and four who have challenging behaviour. The majority are girls and young women (there are three boys), and are aged between five and twenty-six, although the official age range is five to nineteen. Three staff are available at any one time, including at night.

Princess Alice Drive, with its chapel, school, workshop, farm and bakery and staff houses was not untypical of its time: long-stay hospitals often had the same facilities and exhibited the same self-sufficiency. In addition, the NCH Sisters training school at one time shared the site. Behind Premier Way stand the fields that once surrounded Princess Alice Drive. Had the recession of the early 1990s not intervened, the land would have been sold for further development and the Premier Way bungalows would have been part of a housing estate. As it is, the fields are still there, and, apart from the petrol station and superstore, Premier Way, at the moment, looks a little set apart.

Inside the bungalows, there is intimacy, warmth and dignity. The interior of Number 3 indicates that its residents have challenging be-haviour. In the sitting-room, with its brightly-painted walls and stripped pine, vaulted ceiling, the television set and radio set are out of reach. None of the bedrooms is lavishly furnished. In one there is only a bed with duvet (no sheets), for the girl whose room it is tears things up. The walls show one or two marks of her behaviour (though, surprisingly, elsewhere in the buildings there are no marks on the walls, no signs of scuffing). Her wardrobe is kept in another room. A Venetian blind has to be protected by double glazing. Inside Number 1 it is entirely different. Each bedroom shows the individuality of those who live there—photographs, posters, attractive pine furniture.

For both sets of youngsters, there are specially designed bathrooms, wall-rails, and wide doors for wheelchair access. Those with special needs have individually made armchairs in their rooms and comfortable, individually designed ones on wheels to use elsewhere in the building. The décor of these bungalows must be more than functional for these children, as for any child: careful consideration is given to colour schemes which have an important effect on everyday life, behaviour and peace of mind. Welcome, comfort, quality, individual care are the hallmarks of Premier Way.

The key to the work of the project are the individual personal plans drawn up by staff, parents and others to target the individual needs and particular behaviours of the children and young adults. It is important that parents should see what will be done, that they agree to it, and will implement the care plan when the child is at home. In the same way, the plan has to be adhered to at either the special school or the day centre which the youngsters attend.

Vinod Verma, the project manager, says: 'The key is consistency, not believing that you can change everything in two weeks, but needing to identify two or three behaviours, in the case of those of the residents who have challenging behaviour, and working to change that.

'By consistency, I mean ensuring that there is a pattern in what they do and what is done with them from getting up in the morning to going to bed at night; seeing that it is all done in the same way. For example, if there is a toiletting programme or a feeding programme, it means making sure that staff stick to them, whoever that member of staff happens to be, or wherever—in the school or here—they happen to be. And it means ensuring also that the parents know that and stick with it. Likewise, if there's a particular behaviour, then we have to ensure that it is dealt with consistently by whoever is there at the time.'

Only one of the children has no parental contact, but the relationship with parents differs: one child goes home for the day every Thursday; another goes home for the weekend every fortnight; while another never goes home, but his mother visits him regularly. Work with one youngster has progressed to the extent that it is hoped that he will be able to return to live permanently with his parents. As well as involving parents actively in the care of their children, there is also a parents' support group. Vinod Verma says: 'I want to offer a service where parents feel that they are welcome because it's easy for those parents to feel uncomfortable in somewhere like Premier Way because they are entrusting their child to us and they can very easily and understandably have feelings of guilt or failure.'

He says that the work with children and young people with challenging behaviour is 'physically and emotionally demanding' because no one has the answer to how it can be managed. Staff work forty-five hours a week, and while their basic salaries are higher than they could expect in a social services department or a health authority, they also get additional payment for extra hours.[2]

Staff are supported by regular supervision, team and staff meetings, and close working with other staff—the local community learning difficulties team or special school staff. When a behaviour modification programme is being introduced, the team manager of the local authority's support services team is on hand to work with staff involved in the programme and offer additional support.

Premier Way is based on a realistic assessment of the abilities of those who live there: there is little chance that the residents could live independently (unlike many disabled people), and even their participation in their home—in the choice of décor, for example—is inevitably limited. But the use of the key worker idea—where a staff member is assigned to an individual—allows for as much individual attention and meeting individual needs as possible.

Vinod Verma sees what is on offer as 'an appropriate and a quality service'. He also sees it as being flexible. At the moment, everyone who comes to Premier Way does so with the intention that they will live there permanently. But, he says, Premier Way, like the rest of social services, has to be open to changing ideas and needs. 'Our aim,' he says 'must be a flexible service that meets local needs. Our intention is to be responsive. Our emphasis now is to provide care in the homes, on a long-term basis, but in five years' time—who knows? The challenge to NCH Action For Children is to be responsive to local needs.'

If a revival in the economy saw those nearby fields covered with housing and Premier Way less out on a limb, it would take considerably more than that to ensure adequate services for its residents being offered, other than by NCH Action For Children. Day care, for those above the school-leaving age (which is nineteen for young people in special schools), is a major problem.

Day care should be on offer five days a week: at the moment all that can be obtained is two. When a young person is seventeen, plans must be made to see where they will live once they leave Premier Way, but again this is not so easily found. Vinod Verma and his staff have looked at local authority, private and voluntary services as far away as Wales (though their aim is to find accommodation as local as possible) but rarely find anywhere that matches the quality of what is being currently enjoyed. At this time only some of the residents are of an age when that change has to be made. It is possible that the future demands flexibility from NCH Action For Children, and that Premier Way and places like it will be seen as part of a continuum of care, providing day services and accommodation for the next stage of life.

Vinod Verma can see that this might be so; but, ideally, he says, those living in Premier Way ought to go to a different environment—'it's natural and normal for that to happen to everyone'—otherwise there is the danger of creating a total care system, replicating some of the worst aspects, albeit with infinitely higher standards, of institutional care in a community setting.

Just as the Children Act 1989 is about partnership with parents, which NCH Action For Children is putting into practice in Premier Way, so the community care legislation, implemented in 1993, is about meeting individual needs through specially designed 'packages of care', rather than offering standardized, take-it-or-leave-it services. But if local authorities don't have the resources to offer the day care or the adult accommodation that meets the needs of children and young people who live in somewhere like Premier Way, then such planning doesn't have much meaning. Premier Way offers some of the best examples of service for children and young people with severe disabilities. But the empty fields behind it and the lack of services in the community show how reliant are those who live and work there on circumstances entirely beyond their control.

10 | A new world: from 1969 to 1994

In 1969 the National Children's Home began its centenary year with a new principal. Gordon Barritt was a Methodist minister who had come into the organization in 1957 with responsibility for aftercare work.[1] He could look back on the hundred years of the Home's existence as a century of steady progress bequeathed by his predecessors. The organization's domain now covered forty-nine children's homes; it had 2,650 children in its care; it was a long-established adoption agency; and its income that year reached £1,944,679. In 1969, later concerns like child abuse had still to seep into the consciousness of social workers, let alone that of the public. Matters such as equal opportunities for disadvantaged groups, the needs of children from black and ethnic minority backgrounds, and children's rights were not yet to the forefront of its concerns. Significantly, while fostering and adoption were long-established, residential care was still a prized and widely used part of welfare provision.

The world turned upside down

But within twenty-five years, the world within which agencies like the Home worked had been turned upside down—old solutions were questioned, new ones sought; new services arose to meet problems as yet not fully explored; reorganizations shook both health and welfare systems; new philosophies and methods of caring, and of attitudes toward those who were cared for, made themselves felt. There were, literally, dozens of pieces of legislation which directly or indirectly affected the work of voluntary agencies—those affecting social security benefits; the education needs of disabled children; taking children into care; dealing with young offenders, and many more.

The family changed: the proportion of single parents with dependent children more than doubled—from 8 per cent in 1971 to 18 per cent twenty years later. (In the last fifteen years the number of people living in poverty has grown; the hardest hit being families with young children.) Over the twenty-five years divorce rates went up two-fold and the numbers of couples cohabiting rose to one in three. Users of services, too, came into their own: they were no longer content to be the recipients of services but wanted a say in shaping them. In particular, young people who were in care gained legal rights, and procedures for complaints had to be established.

No organization could fail to be affected as the contours of its world were drawn and redrawn, least of all the Home. It too underwent its own reorganization. Toward the end of Gordon Barritt's sixteen-year tenure as principal, it began a massive reshaping which would not end until Barritt's successor-but-one, Tom White (whose appointment was to be a part of those changes), was in post. Barritt and his successor Michael Newman began with the dismantling of the old board of management, investing much of its power in the principal's job and creating a streamlined senior staff structure. The position of child care secretary, like other board jobs, went, and the new post of director of social work was created.

Tom White's recruitment to that job in 1985 augured even more radical things to come. For fifteen years he had been the innovative director of Coventry social services department, a shrewd politician, one of the two best known and most forceful directors of social services. Not only had he raised Coventry to national notice. Fifteen years before he had been one of those who had led the Seebohm Implementation Group, a pressure lobby which had campaigned for the Seebohm Report, which was to lead to the revamping of welfare services into the all-embracing social services departments in 1971. He was a leading member of his profession through the Association of Directors of Social Services, at one time holding its presidency. He was a well-known Labour supporter, and it had been Barbara Castle's wish to appoint him to head of the social work side of the Department of Health and Social Services, when she became Secretary of State.[2] If he could be coaxed from Coventry and such extra-curricular activities, the Home meant business.

When Michael Newman retired in 1990, Tom White was appointed principal with the additional new title of 'chief executive'. The appointment represented a significant break with tradition: he was the first lay person to be appointed to head the organization. The restructuring continued with even greater force until the organization was finally reshaped into a modern, businesslike voluntary agency ready and able to swim in the uncertain waters that now engulfed welfare in general and the voluntary agencies in particular.

The 'mixed economy' of welfare in the 90s

One of the ships being floated on those waters was that governments, through policy statements and funding arrangements, were giving new emphasis to the idea of state and voluntary agency working together. Government money had, even in Gordon Barritt's day, been pumped into voluntary bodies. Examples of this had been the Department of Health's Intermediate Treatment Initiative in 1983 and the Under-5s Initiative (see below). Two years before Barritt's retirement the £5 million a year income which the organization gained from voluntary giving was dwarfed by the £12 million from local authorities, the largest receipt taken by any voluntary agency. But that was a taste of things to come.

Voluntary agencies were no longer seen as complementary to state and local authority endeavour, but partners in it. The phrase which would come to be adopted, with the reforms under the NHS and Community Care Act in the early 90s, would be 'the mixed economy of welfare' or 'welfare pluralism'. The government's intention was that the independent sector of voluntary and private organizations should play a larger part in providing services, with local authorities less as providers of services and more as purchasers, regulators, monitors and inspectors of them (see chapter 11).

The two most visible signs of the changes as they affected NCH (although they could be well seen even when Gordon Barritt was in post), were, first, that it had ceased to be an organization primarily offering residential care. Second, the children for whom it had cared, the 'sunshine babies'—the smiling blond, white, curly-haired children, whose photographs had in some ways symbolized the fund-raising of an earlier generation—were nowhere to be seen. Abortion, the easier availability of contraception (and, especially, the birth control pill), the decision of young unmarried women to keep their children rather than to place them for adoption, signalled an entirely different population of children available for adoption: they were older, and they might have a disability, or suffer emotional problems or come from a black or ethnic minority family.

NCH was not alone in experiencing these changes. All the big child care organizations, such as Barnardo's and The Children's Society, were forced to rethink their roles. It is arguable that the changes which the 'Big Three' underwent were more painful and difficult than that of smaller organizations as they carried with them a longer history and more organizational baggage. They had to take on another role, or rather rediscover one. When Stephenson had begun his work, he was not only rescuing the homeless young people he found on the streets. The kind of care which he was offering—residential homes—was a reaction against the kind of place commonly provided—large, institutional and barrack-like. In the middle years of the century that reforming zeal had lain dormant in the Home. Now it was time to regain that ground, as a reforming body which also pioneered services.

The home front: residential care

It is difficult to pinpoint the beginnings of discontent about residential care for children. When Stephenson opened the Home, by the standards of the time and up to 1914, residential care provided good care relative to life outside: children were sheltered, and enjoyed better health, clothing and food. But with growing prosperity, higher standards of living generally, and the fall in infant mortality figures, institutional care came to be seen as a second best.[3] As long ago as 1946 the Curtis Committee had seen residential care as the least favoured option for children unable to live with their natural families (see chapter 7). And in the last twenty years the falling numbers of children needing to go into such care has contributed to its decline.

The introduction of imaginative adoption and specialized fostering for 'hard to place' children, welfare benefits and other kinds of support that help families to stay together and other forms of care like intermediate treatment, all drained the pool from which children were drawn. In the past, for many children residential care had been seen as a channel for securing employment for them—young women into service, young men into the armed services or the Merchant Navy—but this was no longer the case. As with other kinds of residential care (like that for people with a mental illness and those with a learning difficulty), research was showing that residential care did not bring all the benefits claimed for it by its evangelists and might also have disadvantages for those who experienced it.[4]

So it was that various streams of discontent ran into the flood which was to bring about the decline in residential care. For most children, residential care was far less preferable to fostering or adoption. Local authorities became increasingly reluctant to make use of it. Modern child care practice was also to try not to place children far from their family home (when they had one). The need to use resources economically also meant that local authorities had first to fill their own homes before seeking out vacancies in those of voluntary agencies.

The consumer voice began to be heard and it was often critical. There was a powerful movement among young people who had been in care to voice their views about the standards of care, their lack of rights, and their prospects (or lack of them) after they left care. This movement was first sparked by the National Children's Bureau with its publication in 1977 of *Who Cares?: Young People in Care Speak Out* and took off with most force with the founding of the (now defunct but once influential) National Association of Young People in Care. Last but not least, the research published in 1973 as *Children Who Wait* [5] provided powerful evidence that the first few weeks in care were crucial in a child's rehabilitation and that children left languishing in residential care had a poor prognosis of ever returning home.

While the last twenty-five years saw a decline in residential care as a result of these trends, with the passing of the years a more balanced view gradually came to recognize that such care could be part of a wider spectrum of services. Residential care became more specialized. It catered for children and young people whose needs, for whatever reason, could not be met in the community. Sometimes it was used only in the short term or for emergencies.

NCH's commitment was to a belief that the best interests of most children are met in their natural family, or, where that is not possible, in a substitute family. Residential care can be helpful for some kinds of children: those who have said that they do not wish to be fostered; those awaiting family placements, or whose experiences of fostering have been negative. Residential care can be an option for children who have been abused in their own family or a substitute family when placement with another family is undesirable. Some children, because of their personal and social needs, may require sophisticated and expert treatment available only in a residential setting (see sections on Premier Way and Penhurst School, chapter 9). Residential care may also help brothers and sisters to stay together when fostering would mean their separation. Some families need the break which respite care can offer, and there are those children for whom containment and treatment in secure accommodation is required when they are a danger to themselves and others.

An example of the shape of the new residential care was shown when in 1991 NCH opened the first of its three residential family centres, combining under one roof the best of both kinds of care. The intention of these—they are all in London—is to allow children with severe needs to stay with their families. There are seven self-contained flats available to families in need. These families have had a long history of difficulties, perhaps having been unsuccessful attenders at day centres or unresponsive to other kinds of help. Here they can receive support from their own social worker, who works with NCH Action For Children staff, to develop family and parenting skills while remaining in their local areas. They stay in their new homes for six months. Each family starts with a four-week assessment to see what it needs. Then they may be offered play work, individual counselling, group work and family therapy that can involve everything from teaching parents how to play with their children to budgeting and looking at the parents' own relationships and childhood.

But while the new, specialized forms of residential care were evolving, the day-to-day reality was that residential care had become the poor relation in welfare. In the last few years in particular, there has been a succession of scandals, often involving the abuse of children, followed by inquiry reports, all pointing to a dis-ease within residential care and the need for the development of a comprehensive strategy. But each crisis met with its own, often differing, solution from the government. There were arguments about the best forms of training for residential staff, but the sorry fact remained that, whatever training might be desirable, only a small percentage of those who ran homes had a qualification. This was even more evident in the levels of unqualified staff.[6] (NCH Action For Children had been an exception to this due to its the long enthusiasm for trained managers and staff, first encouraged by Stephenson).

One response to this crisis was the coming together in 1993 of a group of child care experts, with Tom White as chairperson, in the Advancement of Residential Child Care or ARCC. This was a pressure group, brought into being by concerns about the lowly status of residential care and the failure to do much fundamental to cure its long-standing and well-publicized ills. ARCC wanted to see being in care as a positive experience, and the new attitude to residential care shared not only by the government but by local authorities and voluntary agencies also. In its initial statement ARCC stressed the importance of a knowledgeable and committed management for residential child care; full participation by children and parents in a partnership with those who ran services; comprehensive staff development and training; and staff recruitment policies which improved selection procedures, and gave adequate staffing levels, and better salaries and conditions.

Within a few months the government, seeing that it had to do something in the face of scandals, and reports which no one appeared to be heeding, announced a child care support force that would visit local authorities, monitor practice and seek to develop new ideas. ARCC greeted the force's announcement enthusiastically, even if it expressed doubts about its too narrow terms of reference.[7] But it was far too early for ARCC to pack its bags. The support force had decades of neglect to tackle.

No roof over their heads: youth homelessness

Young people huddled under makeshift bedding, sleeping in doorways or begging in the streets of big cities were one of the most visible symbols of deepening deprivation and the widening gap between the poor and the better-off in the 1980s. More than a century after the NCH came into being Stephenson's 'little nation of vagrant children' still remained to be conquered.

Youth homelessness had been exacerbated by a government decision in 1988 to deny social security benefits to sixteen- to eighteen-year-olds. This was done in the belief that children should be living at home. It assumed that they did not need as much to live on as someone who was older. The decision ignored the fact that many children were estranged from their parents. Many had left home because of abuse. Indeed, a third of the 150,000 sixteen- to nineteen-year-olds who are homeless each year have been in care.[8] This is but one aspect of their story—they need more than just a roof over their heads. Their very vulnerability means that they need parenting support, which, in the absence of natural parents to offer it, needs to be provided by workers in projects for homeless youngsters. Too often children can leave care not only with nowhere to go and no support, but lacking also the elementary knowledge of how to cope and look after themselves. Youngsters who, for most of their lives, have been supervised over the slightest thing are hardly likely to be able to run their own home, let alone navigate the wider and largely unknown world.

There is also a disproportionate number of young homeless youngsters from black and ethnic minority backgrounds. Little information exists on why this should be so (although a disproportionate number of such youngsters are also in care). Discrimination in both housing and employment indicates that a higher percentage may well be homeless, as these two features are major contributory factors.

Denied benefits, many young people are not able to find a job or a place on a Youth Training Scheme. And even if they are lucky enough to find either, the chances that the income (especially on YTS) will allow them to set up their own home are minimal. In 1990 a report based on a MORI poll commissioned by the government found that over half the sixteen- to seventeen-year-olds who had been sleeping rough said that they needed to beg, steal or sell drugs to survive.[9]

Although, under the Children Act 1989, local authorities have a duty to assist young people leaving care up to the age of twenty-one (previously their responsibility ended when the young person was eighteen), provision remains patchy. NCH's own research in 1987 highlighted the lack of work by local authorities in the field. In that year over a fifth of housing authorities which responded to a survey said that they did not regard as vulnerable 'a girl open to sexual and financial exploitation'. Half those authorities did not regard as vulnerable a young homeless person with 'no parents and no support'.[10] And so, they overlooked the needs of those like the young man who said:

> Out of care and with nowhere else to go, I ended up in London. I had no idea what I was up against.

Or another who said:

> After the children's home, social services found me a bedsit, but I hated it. I had no idea how to look after myself. I hated being on my own with nothing to do and no one to talk to.

There was the young woman who said:

> They said I went into care then because my father couldn't cope. It was also because he had begun hitting us a lot. He didn't care much about us, he drank a lot, and didn't look after us or pay us much attention. I was relieved in a way to get away.

Another young woman said:

> From the time I was only a few years old, mum started to beat me up. It seemed that every time she broke up with one of her boyfriends, or they hit her, she would take it out on me.[11]

NCH Action For Children provides two kinds of projects for vulnerable and homeless young people. The first gives shelter to youngsters who would otherwise sleep rough. The other type of project is that for vulnerable young people leaving either care or their family homes, who might otherwise become homeless (see sections on the Bristol Housing Project and the Calderdale Leaving Care Project, chapter 9). The organization runs nineteen projects for young people who are homeless and/or are leaving care and being helped into independent living. What they offer was summed up by the young man who said: 'The staff here were like parents to me. A lot of kids don't know how to show their emotions because their parents don't know how to either. It was so important knowing that there was someone who was there for me.'

In a series of reports and campaigns in the last decade, some on its own, some in conjunction with other charities, NCH Action for Children has worked to reverse the law on benefit changes. It sought to abolish the 170 year old Vagrancy Act, which caused young people sleeping on the streets to be at best harassed and at worst brought before the courts. In 1993 it called, in a report, for the government to set up a company to purchase some of the estimated 270,000 empty homes to house homeless people.[12] Although councils were making less use of bed and breakfast accommodation for homeless families, the report said that the alternatives—hostels, short-life flats and refuges—were hardly much better. Twenty thousand children were housed in this way, with another 23,000 in bed and breakfast hotels. The report stated: 'The long-term use of temporary accommodation affects residents' health, children's education and personal relationships'.

Family secrets: sexual and physical abuse

There are dreadful connecting currents which run through the lives of many of the children and young people with whom NCH Action For Children works. Abused, they leave home and end up sleeping rough, or they go into care and on leaving care the streets offer the only 'home'. Although the physical abuse of children stretches back to ancient times, it was only in 1946 that a radio-logist, John Caffey, noted multiple fractures in the long bones of six children suffering from chronic subdural haematoma. But while he is credited as initiating the medical world's 'first great concern', the state of knowledge at the time was such that he remained mystified as to the cause. As then, one difficulty which still faces those working in the field is a reluctance by many people—professional as well as lay—to actually accept that such things can happen. It is too painful to consider what parents may be capable of doing to their children.

The first real raising of public and professional consciousness came when Henry Kempe, an American doctor, and his colleagues coined the phrase 'the battered baby syndrome' in 1962. However, it was not until 1974 that public and professionals alike were forced to sit up and listen when the report into the death of Maria Colwell at the hands of her foster father was published. This was the first of literally dozens of inquiry reports into the deaths of children, some of which found grave fault with the actions of social services departments and their employees, as well as with other professionals such as health visitors and GPs. It also marked the point when child abuse went to the top of the welfare agenda. [13]

Though physical abuse has remained a constant concern for the past twenty years, new forms have come to light. After physical abuse and neglect came sexual abuse, followed by allegations of ritual (officially called 'network') abuse. In 1991 NCH published a report that revealed yet another face—the claim, based on a number of statistical analyses, that one in three children who are sexually abused may be abused by other children, some as young as three years of age.[14] A second NCH report published at the time, on work funded by the Department of Health, supported the findings, and the report itself quoted earlier studies like that published the previous year in *The Journal of Child Law* which had found that 34 per cent of sexual abuse cases involved a child or young person as the abuser. When the report appeared Tom White referred back to the strands which historically have made up child abuse:

> *In the seventies, people found it difficult to believe that adults would batter children. In the eighties, sexual abuse was met with denial and disbelief. In the nineties, we must now face the fact that some children abuse other children.* [15]

It is impossible to assess the numbers of children who suffer from abuse of different kinds. Like rape, levels of reporting have increased which pose the question of whether or not there has been an actual increase in incidence. But in 1988 figures showed that 6,300 children aged nought to sixteen were sexually abused in some way in England and Wales. This is very likely an underestimate of the figures. Various research studies indicate that the incidence of child abuse lies somewhere between 1 and 10 per cent of the UK child population, which means that more than 100,000 children are likely to be abused.[16] Abuse can cause immediate trauma. But it can also have much longer-term consequences not apparent at the time, leading to emotional and psychological problems for the victims, which can make it difficult to form ordinary relationships in later life. One fact which has come to the fore in the last ten years or so is that those who abuse were often abused themselves when children.

NCH Action For Children has worked with abused children and their families in a number of ways. Telephone counselling lines have been established; individual counselling is offered; young people who have left home because of abuse find support and shelter in independent living projects (see above), and there are specialist residential projects, like the Chine in north London. Similarly, family centres also deal with the problem, along with the range of their other concerns (see below). Sometimes specialist foster-parents are found to offer the sensitive parenting required for children whose own natural parents have abused them.

In 1992 the organization took another step forward in the work by opening the first network of specialist treatment centres for sexually abused children and their families, which had been piloted two years previously in Glasgow (see chapter 9). Run in partnership with local and health authorities, and, in some cases, other voluntary agencies, NCH Action For Children now has fifteen such projects—thirteen offering treatment, one engaged in research and one offering residential care—and one more due to open.

Help offered at the centres is available to the child, as well as brothers and sisters and the (non-abusing) parent. It may include specialist counselling, play therapy (where children, using play, can be helped to express their emotions), and psychotherapy and psychiatric help. Families can also be worked with as a group to help them come to terms with what has happened and to repair relationships which have been damaged or distorted by abuse. The abuser can be included in this but only with the consent of family members and only at a time when, if at all, they feel strong enough for it.

The initiative was coupled with a new research project based at Guy's Hospital, London. Most children on local authority 'at risk' registers do not receive the specialist treatment which the centres can offer, but even though NCH Action For Children dedicated £4 million to the venture, it knows that it alone cannot meet all needs. Thus, at the time of launching the network, it also called on the government to put up £6 million which, it was estimated, would at least offer six months' specialist treatment to all those not currently receiving it.

Lock 'em up?: the young and the law

Few issues generate so much heat and create so little light as that of dealing with young offenders. From the halcyon liberal days of 1969 when the Children and Young Persons Act switched emphasis from punishment to treatment, and saw families having a critical role in working with youngsters who found themselves on the wrong side of the law, there were forces working against it. Large parts of the legislation were not implemented as the resources were not available. Within less than a decade the Act was effectively a dead letter, although it was some years before it was replaced on the statute book.

One of the first measures of the incoming Conservative government of 1979, with its electoral pledges about law and order, was to introduce so-called 'short, sharp shock' treatment. There were warnings that these glasshouse regimes—where young people (usually young men) would be locked up and given a diet of hard physical labour and military-style drill—would not work unless the aim was to produce a new generation of physically fit young criminals. The government persisted with its policy. The scheme was soon abandoned: it had no effect on juvenile crime rates (indeed, one study showed that 70 per cent of detainees reoffended within two years) but, importantly, it was criticized by the very staff who ran it. The Prison Officers' Association said that they had turned out 'fit young burglars able to run faster than the police'. This seemed to have a (temporary) sobering effect on the Home Office, whose own research unit had for years been pointing to the deleterious effect of locking up youngsters.

Then came a period of 'diversionary' measures, aimed to keep young people out of custody, and indeed out of the courts. All evidence shows that for most youngsters who cross with the law, their offence tends to be an isolated episode. To bring them through the courts is to give them a criminal record and bring them that much nearer to embarking on a criminal career. Thus, cautioning proved successful in the aim of keeping many out of the courts.

For those who did come to court, the government urged magistrates to consider, first and foremost, non-custodial sentences together with efforts to address offending behaviour (a requirement which became law under the Criminal Justice Act 1991). While alternatives to custody, diversion and emphasis on cautioning continue to be a strong component of government policy on juvenile offenders, renewed concern about a so-called 'hard core' of persistent young offenders (especially those under the age of criminal responsibility) has given new wind to those who regard other kinds of policy as 'soft'. And so the latest government measures to 'crack down' on young offenders seem to bring Conservative measures around full circle fourteen years after the 'short, sharp shock', with secure training centres, the so-called 'child gaols'.

NCH, together with other children's charities, publicly protested that irrational and wrong decisions would be made in the climate that was building up. In a letter to the national press, Tom White of NCH, Nicholas Hinton, director-general of Save the Children Fund, Ian Sparks, director of The Children's Society and others said that the 'general climate of hostility toward young people which has developed in recent weeks... is an unhelpful background with which to introduce new measures to deal with juvenile crime.' They continued:

> *... there is a danger that all the lessons learned in recent years about the clear link between juvenile crime and high reoffending rates will be lost. Schemes to prevent young people being drawn into the criminal justice system, and to confront those who have offended with the consequences of their offending, have proved far more successful than custody in preventing reoffending.*

They added that measures should be effective, not merely punitive, and that to deal with the small numbers of persistent offenders there could be a small increase in local authority secure accommodation if current provision was inadequate. But the most extraordinary fact to which they drew attention was that the ink was hardly dry on the statute book for the Children Act 1989 (implemented in 1991) and the Criminal Justice Act (implemented in late 1992) before their untried provisions were under attack.[17]

What the government was proposing was a new generation of Borstals and approved schools which NCH, together with thirty-five other voluntary and statutory organizations, publicly came out against. These earlier institutions had been abolished because they proved ineffective: they had a bad record on reconvictions. Some brought even more serious charges against them. The criminologist Professor Terence Morris, who had worked in the old system, opposing the government's plans, said that the old regimes were often marked by 'staff brutality ... accompanied by bullying from fellow inmates, to be followed by nocturnal sexual abuse'.[18] Now they were being taken out of some long-forgotten back drawer in the Home Office, dusted off and sold by ministers to the public as part of the new offensive against young offenders.

Such was the opposition to the scheme that a new alliance came into being with a breadth of representation not often seen: NCH was lined up with the Prison Reform Trust, the Law Society, the Association of Chief Probation Officers, the Justices' Clerks Society, the Association of Directors of Social Services, and others. The statement by Stephen Shaw of the Prison Reform Trust that politicians were 'fanning the flames of public anxiety' over juvenile offenders seemed borne out when Michael Jack, the Home Office minister, admitted not only that there was no conclusive statistical evidence that the increase in crime was the responsibility of juvenile offenders, but that the government's initiative 'largely rested on anecdotal evidence from police and magistrates'.[19]

What are the facts about young offenders? The most remarkable is that while overall, the UK, like most Western industrial countries, has experienced a rising crime rate, there has been a decline in offences by young people (those under seventeen). In 1980, 175,800 juveniles in England and Wales were cautioned or found guilty of indictable offences. Ten years later the figure was 110,900—a fall of 37 per cent. Of every 100,000 young men aged 10 to 16, 4,999 were found guilty or cautioned in 1980, against 4,072 in 1990, with particularly significant falls for the under-14s. In addition, much juvenile crime is non-violent. In 1990, 60 per cent concerned theft or handling stolen goods, 17 per cent burglary and only 10 per cent violence.[20]

NCH Action For Children has long been involved with young offenders and had at one time industrial schools, reform schools and approved schools within its charge. Almost all its projects—family centres, counselling services, leaving care projects—have done some work with young people on the wrong side of the law. In 1983 its work in the field expanded significantly when it became the largest voluntary sector investor in the Department of Health and Social Services' Intermediate Treatment Initiative, which made available £15 million to voluntary agencies to set up community-based provision for juvenile offenders over four years. Virginia Bottomley, later Secretary of State for Health and herself a former social worker, referred to the work as bringing about a 'sea change in the way we respond to juvenile offenders'.[21]

Ten years later NCH still ran twelve such projects but more recently had sought to transfer the success of the initiative to the young adult age group, initiating innovative partnership projects with five probation services. It has fifteen projects for young offenders in England and Wales and eight in Scotland (see section on the West Suffolk Youth Justice Centre, chapter 9). One of these, the Hampshire Young Offender Community Support Scheme, places offenders between sixteen and twenty-one in foster families, to give them, as one worker said, 'a chance to be a child again'. In its first two years, thirty-five young people received the intense but informal support which they could only get by living with a family. The worker also said: 'When they [the young person] go into a family they are often unable to accept responsibility for their actions, but after a year we can challenge them about their behaviour without them running away.' A study by the Dartington Research Unit found that more than half of those on the scheme stopped offending, a significantly higher success rate than the custodial alternative.[22]

A poor deal: families, parents and poverty

In 1948 the Children Act set the future tone (if not always the practice) for social work with families when it stated:

> *To keep the family together must be the first aim, and the separation of a child from its parents can only be justified when there is no possibility of securing adequate care for a child in his own home.*[23]

In 1980 a committee, under Professor Roy Parker of the University of Bristol, saw the prevention of children going into care as best done by strengthening the family. It wanted a service which would assist 'parents in their task of child care'.[24] For parents to be involved in day care would allow them to be taught parenting skills and build up confidence. It acknowledged the role of poverty in contributing to family breakdown, but the solutions which it proffered were those of parenthood classes, social work with couples, sympathetic support from social workers and health visitors, group care for depressed mothers and their children, day care which involved mothers, and a philosophy of shared care, which, nine years later, was to be enshrined in the Children Act. Eight years before the Parker report Sir Keith Joseph, when Secretary of State for Social Services, had made an influential speech about 'the cycle of deprivation'.[25] Thus, the times were ripe to see how that cycle could be broken.

With 'rescue' no longer fashionable and the tide turning away from residential care, preventive work through day care was one new strand which bodies such as the Home could pioneer and adopt. There were, of course, reasons, other than the need for a new role, why it should respond to the tenor of the times. As a Christian organization, linked to the Methodist Church, it placed great emphasis on family life. Parent education and keeping families together have become two of the hallmarks of its work.

The Home was quite explicit that poor parenting was one reason why families sought its help and needed social work intervention. A discussion document published in 1981 stated:

> *It follows then that unless the home situation and quality of care can be improved the effects of any centre-based help given to children are going to be limited. If the home situation and patterns of parental care are going to be influenced to the benefit of the child it equally follows that direct ongoing involvement with parents is essential to the work of the centre...*[26]

But one commentator has argued that the organization found itself facing two ways.[27] First, as a reforming body in welfare provision, critical of government policy which had the effect of deepening poverty, increasing homelessness, and creating unemployment, NCH did not seem able to resist taking the role which successive Conservative governments carved out for it. While it is true that governments of both parties have set the tone of some provision by the kinds of funding which were offered to voluntary bodies, NCH's stance in the face of government financial inducements was the development, from 1985, of strategic five-year plans. These set out the policy and geographical directions which the organization wished to follow. Where government policy coincided with them (as was the case with alternatives to custody), the agency moved into a partnership; where the government's aims were not shared (as with the pressure for voluntary agencies to run secure accommodation for young offenders), it resisted it.

The second way the organization was said to be facing was due more to NCH's own makeup. Its own background had given it both a strongly reformist slant and, at the same time, a stress on the responsibility of the individual. Much as NCH might see other forces—poverty, unemployment, poor housing—adversely affecting families, it was also not divorced from ideas of family pathology, that families had within them the roots of their crises. Thus, family centres often had a therapeutic role, and tended to cater for certain groups. Those which were 'client-focused' restricted help to a minority of families, even if they did concentrate resources on a particularly needy group of clients.

There is a whole range of problems which afflict families that necessitates a variety of approaches, individual and collective. Three million children wake up each day in families which exist on the breadline[28] and in 1992 local authorities in Britain accepted 167,000 households as homeless, and a further 90,000 applied but were unsuccessful[29]. And the poor have become poorer. In October 1991 all families with children received less financial support than they did thirty years before, with the exception of those with one child under eleven. Keeping families together has required more than homilies from politicians about 'family values'. The forces undermining families are powerful.

NCH Action For Children has a network of services aimed specifically at families. They range from debt counselling to mediation services (of which it is the single largest provider), which help parents who are separating sort out responsibilities for their children and their financial arrangements as amicably as possible (see section on Greater Manchester Mediation Service, chapter 9). It has more than 100 family centres and community self-help projects. Many families have only one parent (usually the mother), who may attend a family centre for a whole variety of reasons which mostly tend to belie the claim that NCH Action For Children is offering either one source of help (therapeutic) or another (tackling poverty through, say, welfare rights advice). The mother may want help with child care, social contact, advice and support, or to make use of the centre's facilities.

Work varies but there are three kinds of family centre. 'Referred' centres are those to which families come when the main focus is child abuse and protection. It is here where therapeutic work is most likely to be carried out. 'Neighbourhood' centres are an open door to which residents come as users and helpers. 'Integrated' centres provide a mixture of both kinds of work. Family centres can offer holidays and organize outings, and workers, acting as advocates, can accompany residents to social security hearings. Consider a typical user of NCH Action For Children's services:

> Louise, a divorced mother of four, was suffering from depression and panic attacks when she was referred to an NCH family centre by her social worker. Her two youngest children were showing signs of behavioural problems and her oldest boy had just been picked up by the police for shoplifting.
>
> Workers found that much of what had gone wrong in the family arose from anxieties about debt. Louise felt that the strain caused by mounting debts had been one of the main reasons her husband had left her, but the stress of bringing up her children alone and relying on income support had also taken its toll on the whole family.
>
> Bailiffs had come to the house when she couldn't pay her poll tax; the children had not had new clothes or shoes for more than two years and she lived in constant fear of the electricity and gas being cut off.
>
> As well as providing counselling and working with the children, NCH workers helped Louise sort out a realistic family budget. They then helped her write to her creditors with proposals for smaller, regular payments for her debts, which were accepted. They also arranged for her to see a welfare benefit adviser to ensure she was claiming all her entitlements.[30]

A decade after the Home's discussion document had placed great emphasis on the failures of parenting, which made social work intervention necessary, the agency published a policy statement on family centres which stated:

> The advantages of this model [one which combines a client-centred approach with one which reaches out to the whole neighbourhood; ie, the integrated centre] are that open services are less likely to

> *stigmatise those who use them. There is also a strong likelihood that*
> *stress factors and actual or potential abuse are identified at an early*
> *stage. Research has demonstrated that these open centres do reach a*
> *higher proportion of vulnerable families . . . nevertheless client-focused*
> *work should take place in all of them [the centres]. Similarly, whilst*
> *not necessarily being defined as an integrated model, all centres are*
> *involved in the complex task of integrating structured development*
> *work with children, educational partnership work with parents and*
> *collaborative relationships with other agencies.[31]*

While stressing partnership between workers and parents in referred centres, NCH Action For Children also said that in neighbourhood centres 'the power relationship between project workers and parents will certainly be more equal and in some centres, at the extreme end of the continuum, even reversed.' Not only would parents be 'active partners' in promoting their children's well-being, but they might also be involved in planning and running services and in looking at how effective they are. They would be members of centre advisory and management committees, 'and in some cases this may result in a gradual process of empowerment enabling parents to have more control over community resources'[32] (see section on the Beacon Heath Family Centre, chapter 9). Family centres, like other NCH Action For Children projects, have to be sensitive to the ethnic, linguistic and cultural backgrounds of those who use them. So, for example, information and publicity has to be provided in languages spoken in the area; children helped to maintain and value their ethnic identity; food chosen to respect dietary traditions; and steps taken to guard against the dangers of reinforcing and perpetuating the main role of women as being that of unpaid carers. Staff are recruited from a wide range of religious and ethnic backgrounds.

Community work—which seeks to draw people together to work together, to give them power, and 'to promote social justice and tackle deprivation'[33]—is also well established within the organization. Such projects can help people to fight together against poor housing, for better local services, and to run local initiatives, like community centres, groups and play schemes (see section on the Llanrumney Community Project, chapter 9).

A parent who might be involved in a community work project, as well as attending a family centre, might also be one who faced another kind of problem. In 1991 NCH conducted the first nationwide survey of nutrition among low income families. It looked at 354 families with children under five in fifty-three of the organization's family and community centres. One in five parents had gone hungry in the last month (December 1990) because they 'did not have enough money' to buy food. 44 per cent of them said that they had gone short of food in the past year in order that other members of the family should have enough. One in ten children had gone without food in the previous month as there was not enough money for food, and nearly one in four went without food during the previous month because they did not like the food offered—when the family budget is stretched it is not always possible to offer children a choice. Not one of the parents or children in the survey was eating a healthy diet—that is, one recommended by nutritionists for a healthy life. Two-thirds of the children and half the parents had poor diets. Of these, six parents and four children had very poor diets: less than a portion of vegetable a day, when the daily recommended level is three portions.[34]

The government—in the person of the then junior social security minister Anne Widdicombe—denied this evidence of poor nutrition in relation to income, saying that parents did not look for bargains, and were not educated to buy the right food. But what the survey illustrated so starkly was how difficult benefit levels made it for families to have a nutritious balanced diet. Just £5 a week made the difference between a family of three having a healthy or unhealthy diet. But this was a fifth of the total spent every week on food by families living on income support. The average amount spent on food for each person per week in the sample was £10. The national average expenditure spent on food is £11, or 12.4 per cent of household expenditure. The families in the survey spent 35 per cent of their household budget on food.[35]

There is another group of children, whose situation is often exacerbated by poverty—the 360,000 whom it is estimated[36] have a disability, either physical or mental. The true costs of disability are not taken account of and recognized through the benefits system. In a survey in 1994 of eighty-three carers for children with disabilities, two out of three said that they were not managing well financially.[37] During the previous year two in three had drawn on savings, and nearly half borrowed to meet a big expense. One in five had borrowed just to get by. More than four in five had extra costs because of their child's disability and of these, four in five said that extra costs were not met in full by benefits. One in ten had got in debt because of the extra costs and nearly one in ten (one in four of single parents) said they couldn't meet the extra costs.

The survey also found that there were too few support services for children with disabilities—especially those which are preventive—and families were forced to fight for access to them because they were scarce. One mother of a 19-year-old young woman with learning difficulties said:

It is one long battle for this and that. Why do you have to be at the end of your tether before any help is forthcoming? [38]

Although the sample consisted of those who were in touch with the helping services, two in five of them still felt there was a need for respite care, for more speech therapy, physiotherapy, and comprehensive domiciliary services. Respite care was important to both parents and children. An ll-year-old girl with a progressive muscular disease said:

I liked it [respite care] from the beginning—it was a break ... I felt like the only one, but since I went there I realized I wasn't the only one, there are children with all sorts of problems.

Community and family centres are places where parents with disabled children can also come for support, advice and help, and where their children can play, along with non-disabled children. Some centres offer summer play schemes, others are specialist day centres for disabled children and their families to come together (see section on the South Glamorgan Options Project, chapter 9). NCH Action For Children is also heavily involved in offering respite care, which allows families a break or a chance to get away for a holiday. It also runs link schemes that put a family with a child with a disability in touch with another family in the same area who will provide regular care for the child. For those children who, for various reasons, cannot live with their families, residential homes and schools provide specialist education and help (see section on Penhurst School, chapter 9).

The causes of poverty are too deep and too vast for NCH Action For Children or any other voluntary agency to root out. Nor can it, on its own, give help to every family in difficulty, whether that be caused by personal or financial reasons or because of disability. But through its work with families—as in all its work—the organization seeks to help those afflicted by poverty or who face other problems, as well as to campaign on their behalf. Most important are the principles that underlie that work, which recognize the value and worth of each individual—be it child or single mother—and the ways in which those with whom it works can be its partners. Those principles are the paramount welfare of the child, parental responsibility, anti-discrimination, participation, and working to give those who use NCH Action For Children's services some control over their lives.

11 | Today and tomorrow

It took ninety-five years for the National Children's Home to grow from the first home founded by Stephenson to the thirty-four residential homes and eight residential schools in 1964. Even ten years later the continuing, if more modest, growth of the organization had not shown any significant movement away from residential provision. In 1974 there were thirty-nine residential homes and eight residential schools, but only four family centres and three hostels for young people leaving care.

By the time NCH Action For Children came to celebrate its 125th anniversary in 1994 the change was dramatic—there had not only been a vast increase in the number of projects—215 in all—but residential care was now but a small, specialized part of its work. Nearly half the organization's provision was in family and community centres. There were twenty-three independence projects for young people leaving care and young homeless people, twenty-three community-based young offender and youth projects, fifteen counselling, advice and mediation services, and four homefinding services. Treatment centres for sexually abused children had grown to fourteen and there were twenty-one services for children with disabilities. Residential homes and schools, now highly specialized, numbered only twelve.

These changes reflect the general trend in social services: the favouring of alternatives to residential care. A year later and those figures would probably be different. More projects now receive three- to five-year funding, which makes for unpredictability about their future. And while the organization has an annual budget of £50 million and two-thirds of its work is undertaken in partnership with local authorities, this itself is no guarantee that projects can survive, even when their usefulness can be proven. What is not likely to change is the pattern of provision, which has now been established for nearly a decade.

The face of NCH Action For Children has been changed by a gradual process; at times change has been swift, at others the *status quo* seemed almost to be set in stone. This book has attempted to show the truth of the observation by one historian of voluntary child care services, Roy Parker, when he wrote:

> *Today's problems, policies and controversies cannot be understood without reference to their historical backgrounds. The slate is rarely, if ever, wiped clean. Inasmuch as the care of separated children, or of children at risk, is set within legal, financial and organisational frameworks, it is subject to the continuities and constraints that they embody as well as to the interests which they reflect, create and sustain. Ideas may seem to be new but a little exploration in the past will often reveal their antecedents, different in detail perhaps, but surprisingly similar in their essential characteristics. The current social ills which give rise to the need for child care services seem to bear little resemblance to those of the past, yet can be found to display remarkable likenesses once more is understood about their root causes. However far-reaching changes may appear to be, their origins lie in what has gone before. The present is constructed from the past.[1]*

How great is the burden and the benefit of history upon a body like this, which has grown, developed and diversified over 125 years? And what obligations does the present-day NCH Action For Children owe to its antecedents?

One of the most obvious and essential, perhaps, is to its values. NCH Action For Children remains a Christian organization, answerable ultimately to the Methodist Conference in the same way as was Stephenson with the first Children's Home, when the conference set him aside from his circuit obligations to live out his ministry as head of the new organization. But Stephenson's world was a vastly different one in which to live from today's. Few then would have questioned the role of a Christian-based body. The society in which he lived expressed at least nominal attachment to Christianity. Secularism, though a powerful force, did not have the same influence which it has since acquired. A multi-faith society of people from different cultures was not foreseeable. Equal opportunities staff recruitment policies were not even on the agenda. Stephenson sought to raise the children in his care quite explicitly in the Christian religion. For him the

Home would be the child's new family to which it would feel attachment all its life. As he wrote:

> The child needs the education of a well-ordered community; he needs the discipline of school, the workshop, and the drill ground. He needs to be part of a system which will draw forth all his faculties, which will follow him as he goes into life, and guide and guard him through his dangerous path, and which will be a polar point around which his thoughts and memories will revolve all his life.[2]

Now NCH Action For Children has to take account of factors of which its founder never dreamt. The organization states the core values which underpin its purpose of remedying deprivation and enhancing the lives of children, young people and families through high-quality services, as:

> Recognising the unique worth and value of every individual;

> Recognising the capacity of individuals and families to grow in love and develop their potential;

> Commitment to the importance of working to improve social conditions and challenge injustice;

> The responsible use of resources.[3]

The statement goes on to say that these values are a practical expression of Christian teaching and in keeping with the agency's Christian base. But, equally, they are values which will find favour with those of other religions and none who wish to work for NCH Action For Children, or, importantly, given that the agency is not evangelistic, those who wish to work with it.

The implications for equal opportunities policies, for example, of such an inclusive view is that NCH Action For Children aims to offer equal access to posts at all levels in its organization, regardless of race, religious affiliation, marital status, gender, health, disability, sexual orientation or age. There are two exceptions: the principal and chief executive and the pastoral director are required to be members of the Christian church. Tom White was the first chief executive and principal of the seven since Stephenson to be a lay person.

The organization's history can work against it in the way it is perceived by the public, upon whom it relies for a considerable amount of its income. It changed its name from NCH because it believed the initials did not mean much to the public but it is still occasionally referred to as the National Children's Home. This name evokes all the outdated associations of being an organization offering 'homes' to 'orphans'. A change of name is not enough. So what face does it try to present for its fund-raising purposes?

In 1993–94 NCH Action For Children's total income was £47 million, of which £14.5 million was voluntary income (including legacies). How does it extract such sums from a public who every day see appeals in newspapers and on television for worthy causes at home and abroad? It needs its income not only to sustain its work but also to push it further up the fund-raising ladder: it is number thirty-one in the table of fund-raising by British charities. It is the second largest child care charity after Barnardo's. But as a fund-raiser it is in the top five children's charities (these include the Save the Children Fund, most of whose work is overseas). The contribution of members of the Methodist Church remains significant: nearly 40 per cent of its voluntary income is from Methodists, who contribute half the legacies (legacies amounted to nearly £4 million in 1993–94).

Even in the very earliest days Stephenson was producing photographs (with a certain artistic licence) showing children as they were before they came into his care, and afterwards. These were carefully posed studies, intended, successfully, as it turned out, to move his contemporaries' consciences and empty their wallets and purses. His very title—The Children's Home and Orphanage—showed very easily what he did (see introduction).

But while Stephenson had known from the very beginning that he would have to raise money by resorting to photographs and heart-rending stories, over the years the Home came to adopt a less publicly assertive face. Until twenty years ago fund-raising was still largely among members of the Methodist Church and sufficient to meet the size of the organization's work as it then was. While money was being received from trusts and companies there was, until 1982, no co-ordinated effort at corporate fund raising. How successful more sophisticated corporate fund-raising could be is shown in the fact that in 1982 the Home received £50,000 and four years later £750,000 was entering its coffers from such sources. Last year (1993–94) the figure was £2.1 million.

Fund-raising generally has become more professional. Take house-to-house collections. Each September this takes place through the work of local NCH Action For Children (unpaid) secretaries and Methodist churches. But also throughout the year the organization engages in the recruitment by telephone of volunteers to collect house to house, with each volunteer having to take on no more than forty houses. It is known that each collector averages £13. In l993–94 collectively they brought in £2.7 million. Three years previously the sum had been £1.3 million.

For a decade or more, much more professional and sophisticated fund-raising has been a mark of the organization; today it is ever more necessary. Schools, libraries, museums and hospitals— institutions which in the past saw fund-raising as icing on the cake of state and local authority funding—have now entered the fund-raising market in a big way, themselves often employing professional fund-raisers.

NCH Action For Children's ethical stance means it will not accept donations from companies dealing in tobacco and arms, nor from Nestlé because of its much-criticized and aggressive policy of selling baby milks to mothers in the Third World. Neither does it approach brewers for money (although it will accept donations raised by staff fund-raising from them). Set against those with whom NCH Action For Children will not deal, its corporate sponsors are impressive: Texaco, BVA, MFI, Gordon Fraser, Budgens, Supa-drug, Argos, Bell UK, NISSAN, Europa Food, and First National Finance among them.

All professional fund-raisers know that there is not a bottomless pit which they can dip into. But what they have yet to find out—and appeals for disasters in the Third World, as much as for sexually abused children in this country continue to come in—is where the bottom of the pit lies.

61 per cent of NCH Action For Children's income comes from money from local authorities as fees or partnership work and from central government. Current government policies about what the respective roles of local authorities and voluntary agencies should be may change both the role and funding of the agency out of all recognition within a few years. The NHS and Community Care Act, implemented in l993, was the government's seal on, and strategy for, its care in the community policies. In the legis-lation, the role of social services departments is delineated as that of 'enablers' and purchasers of services rather than that of direct providers. What this means in practice will differ from local authority to local authority. And while the government's funding mechanisms are geared to encourage the purchase of services from the independent—voluntary and private— sector, much will also depend on how thriving a sector can be found in each authority's area. Also, the squeeze on local authority budgets means that social services departments are more likely to look at alternative options as a means of providing services at less cost.

However uncertain the future may be, however difficult it is to predict what the pattern of service provision will be in two, three, or five, let alone ten years' time, the extent of the changes has caused both would-be providers and purchasers to reassess traditional approaches and ways of thinking. But the idea that voluntary organizations are sitting waiting for the rich pickings of services which local authorities are no longer able or willing to provide themselves is mistaken. NCH Action For Children, for example, will not enter into contracts unless it does so as a partner and if it believes it can provide an enhanced service. It does not want to sign on the dotted line of a service specification to which it has made no contribution. It is less interested in responding to the needs of social services departments than it is to the needs of children and families in association with those departments. But it is also important for voluntary agencies that, whatever the government's ultimate hope, local authorities do not withdraw entirely as providers, be-coming only approvers of contracts and monitors and inspectors of services, or how else will they understand the type, range and quality of services required?

From the point of view of the voluntary agencies, there is the need to retain their independence and, however welcome greater infusions of central and local government funding may be, a sizeable independent income is one way to ensure continuing independence, rather than becoming arms of government. The development of the NCH Action For Children child sexual abuse treatment network showed the value of independent money for independent action (see chapter 9). Here the organization's agitation for specialist treatment services, the need for which was widely acknowledged, was getting nowhere and so it decided to provide them (in partnership with local authorities) itself.

Whatever may be the future shape of NCH Action For Children, however successful its fund-raising, and wherever the radical shift in the provision of services may take it, some facts continue stubbornly to confront it 125 years after Stephenson converted the stable in south London into a home for the first children.

In the 1990s 28 per cent of children were found to be living in poverty.[4] In 1993, 156,000 young people were found to be sleeping rough,[5] and 41 per cent of homeless young people have been in care. Two-thirds of the rest who have been forced to leave their homes because of eviction, violence, poverty or arguments said that they could only return as a last resort.[6] Four in ten young women who become homeless do so as a result of sexual abuse.[7] Poverty remains a root cause of deprivation and inequality and is as much at the core of NCH Action For Children's concerns in 1994 as it was in 1869.

Thomas Bowman Stephenson could never have comprehended that the body he founded would reach not only through this country but overseas, despite his part in the Canadian emigration project. He would be surprised at the growth of services provided by state and local authorities. But what would strike him most assuredly would be, not only, as Roy Parker noted, that the origins of changes lie in what has gone before,[8] but that so many of the problems he confronted remain to challenge NCH Action For Children in its second century.

Notes

Introduction

1. Roy Parker, *Away from Home: A History of Child Care*, Barnardo's, 1990.

2. Eileen Younghusband, *Social Work in Britain: 1950–1975. A Follow-up Study. Volume 1*, Allen & Unwin, 1978.

3. See, for example, Gillian Wagner, *Children of the Empire*, Weidenfeld & Nicolson, 1982, and Joy Melville and Philip Bean, *Lost Children of the Empire*, Unwin & Hyman, 1980.

1

1. Paul Langford, 'The 18th century', in Kenneth Morgan (editor), *The Oxford Illustrated History of Britain*, Oxford University Press, 1984.

2. As above.

3. J. H. Plumb, *England in the 18th Century*, Penguin Books, 1990.

4. When Methodism was reunited in 1932, embodied within it was the United Methodist Church, which had been formed in 1907 by a union of the Methodist New Connexion, the Bible Christians, and the United Methodist Free Churches. This latter group had itself been an amalgam of a number of smaller Methodist communities which had broken from Wesleyan Methodism for constitutional, not doctrinal, reasons. One of these was the Wesleyan Methodist Association which itself had broken away in 1835–36.

5. William Bradfield, *Life of The Reverend Thomas Bowman Stephenson BA, LLD, DD*, Charles A. Kelly, 1913. Other biographical details in this chapter are from Bradfield unless otherwise stated.

6. Quoted by Peter Fairclough, 'Dickens and the Poor Law', appendix to *Oliver Twist*, Charles Dickens, Penguin Books, 1966.

7. For a vivid picture of the life of the Victorian theatre and its players see especially Claire Tomalin, *The Invisible Woman: The Story of Nelly Ternan and Charles Dickens*, Viking, 1990.

8. Bradfield, as above.

9. Cyril Davey, *A Man for All Children: The Story of Thomas Bowman Stephenson, BA, LLD, DD*, Epworth Press, 1968. Reprinted NCH, 1989.

10. Open-air meetings were a time-honoured part of Methodism which were taken up not only by other non-conformists but also by the Established Church. Owen Chadwick gives the example of Tait, when Bishop of London, surprising people by preaching at an open-air meeting in a working class district. He founded the London Diocesan Home Mission which gave that specific task to clergy (Owen Chadwick, *The Victorian Church*, Volume 2, A & C Black, 1970). Not for nothing was William Booth, founder of the Salvation Army, an adolescent convert to Methodism from the Church of England.

11. Quoted Davey, as above.

12. Quoted, as above.

2

1. William Bradfield, *The Life of Thomas Bowman Stephenson*, Charles H. Kelly. 1913. Quotations in this chapter are taken from Bradfield unless otherwise indicated. Gillian Wagner, in her definitive *Barnardo* (Weidenfeld & Nicolson, 1979) traces the earliest account by Barnardo of his discovery of the boys to an article in *The Christian* in 1872. In this version Barnardo comes upon the urchin Jim Jarvis who shows him the plight of other youngsters. The number found is not given, but when the doctor asks if it is possible that there could be more boys in this situation, his youthful guide is quoted as saying: 'Oh yes sir, lots, 'eaps on 'em! More'n I could count!'

2. Wagner, as above.

3. For a brief but useful history, see Robert Holman, *Trading in Children: A Study in Private Fostering*, Routledge & Kegan Paul, 1973.

4. J.L.& Barbara Hammond, *Lord Shaftesbury*, Frank Cass, 1969.

5. Nehemiah Curnoch, *History of the Children's Home*, quoted, Bradfield.

6. Quoted, Cyril Davey, *A Man for All Children: The Story of Thomas Bowman Stephenson*, Epworth Press, 1968. Reprinted by NCH, 1989.

7. The Sunday regime seems quite liberal for its time and given the religious auspices under which the regime was run. For an example of a dour sabbatarian Sunday, as it afflicted a young person 20 years later and in a home with no formal attachment to religion, see Walter Southgate, *That's the Way it Was: A Working Class Autobiography*, New Clarion Press, 1982.

8. The details of George Oliver are from Terry Philpot, 'Caring about the past', *Community Care*, 17 March 1983, from which other details regarding records in this chapter are also are taken. The NCH Action For Children archives have been removed from its Highbury, London headquarters to the University of Liverpool.

9. Quoted, Bradfield.

10. This was the only case of incest the author came across in a wide but not systematic reading of the records.

11. Roy Parker, *Away from Home: A History of Child Care*, Barnardo's, 1990.

12. As above. Professor Parker states that, on the matter of their use by the Poor Law authorities as emigration agencies, some voluntary agencies had, by the 1890s, become wholly given over to pursuing this policy. One such agency was the Middlemore Homes in Birmingham.

13. *Report of the Care of Children Committee*, HMSO, 1946.

14. Quoted, Bradfield.

3

1. William Bradfield, *Life of the Reverend Thomas Bowman Stephenson, BA, LLD, DD*, Charles H. Kelly, 1913.

2. Gillian Wagner, *Barnardo*, Weidenfeld & Nicolson, 1979.

3. Bradfield, as above.

4. As above.

5. A.W. Mager, 'Juvenile emigration', *The Children's Advocate*, June 1893. A paper given to the conference of the Reformatory and Refuge Union at Exeter, 30 May 1893.

6. Thomas Bowman Stephenson, 'Emigration', *The Children's Advocate*, October 1881.

7. A W Mager, as above. Andrew Doyle (see below), in his report, thought that only babies who could be adopted should go. Canadian social workers eventually realized the dangers of exploitation to which young children could be exposed and after 1924 no child under the age of 14 could be sent to Canada. I am grateful to Dame Gillian Wagner for drawing this to my attention.

8. As above.

9. Joy Parr, *Labouring Children: British Immigrant Apprentices to Canada 1869–1924*, Croom Helm, 1980. Stephenson, quoted by Bradfield, stated that 'adoption' was for children not more than five or six years of age.

10. Gillian Wagner, *Children of the Empire*, Weidenfeld & Nicolson, 1982.

11. Bradfield.

12. As above.

13. Anonymous 'The Canadian connection: The Children's Home in Ontario', NCH Action For Children archives, undated

14. Quoted in Kenneth Bagnell, *The Little Immigrants: Orphans who came to Canada*, MacMillan of Canada, 1980.

15. Quoted in Joy Melville and Philip Bean, *Lost Children of the Empire*, Unwin & Hyman, 1989.

16. Report by Andrew Doyle to the President of the Local Government Board on Emigration of Pauper Children to Canada, Parliamentary

Paper, 1875. Quoted, above.

17. Public Archives of Canada, quoted by Wagner, 1982.

18. 'The Canadian connection', as above.

19. 'Canada branch', *National Children's Home and Orphanage Annual Report*, 1893–94.

20. Melville and Bean, as above.

21. Quoted, above. Dating the first child migration from that to Richmond, Virginia in 1618 and the last to Australia in 1967, Melville and Bean estimate that in all about 150,000 children were sent to various outposts of the empire, and that 11 per cent of today's Canadians are descended from the children sent from England. They also quote an estimate from the Canadian Public Archives in 1988 that the total figure for that country was 90,000. Wagner, 1982, above, writes: 'It is known that between 1870 and 1930, Canada received more than 100,000 children.' Roy Parker (*Away from Home: A History of Child Care*, Barnardo's, 1990) puts the number of children who left Britain in the half century before the First War as 80,000. Most of them would have gone to Canadian farms.

22. John H. Litten, *Our News*, Summer, 1934.

23. 'New homes overseas', *National Children's Home Year Book*, 1950.

24. In fact, Litten had contacted a number of Australian Methodist Church societies. That in Victoria was enthusiastic about rebuilding its children's home in Cheltenham, Melbourne and could do so by attracting an Australian government capital grant by taking children from the UK. (Anonymous, 'Child migration, 1950–55', unpublished paper, NCH Action For Children, 1994.)

25. 'New Homes Overseas', as above.

26. 'Child Migration 1950–55', as above.

27. As above.

28. Quoted, as above.

29. As above.

30. As above.

31. Of the files of 85 of the 91 children who went to Australia which were studied (as above), 28 had one parent dead, with the other parent unable to care for them. Fifteen had been deserted by one or both parents. Six were orphaned. Fifteen children were born to unmarried mothers. Five were in care through neglect and two beyond control. Fourteen of the parents were separated or divorced, with the remaining parent unable to care. Five of the 85 were aged five to eight; eleven, 8–10; seventeen, 10–12; twenty-two 12–14; twenty-four 14–16; and six 16–18. Twenty-nine of the children retained links with the Home including those who sought (and were given) access to their files. Five came back to the UK, four asked to but were refused; and 17 have retained or developed a contact with their families in the UK.

4

1. Quoted, Gordon E. Barritt, *The Edgworth Story*, National Children's Home, 1972.

2. Quoted, as above.

3. William Bradfield, *The Life of Thomas Bowman Stephenson*, Charles H. Kelly, 1913.

4. Quoted, as above.

5. As above.

6. Pat Turner and Jenny Elliott, *Adoption—Reviewing the Record*, NCH, 1992.

7. Roy Parker, *Away from Home: A History of Child Care*, Barnardo's, 1990. This refers to Florence Davenport Hill's book, *Children of the State: The Training of Juvenile Paupers*, Macmillan, 1868. Nevertheless, fostering had had its own 'baby farming' scandals, which led from the founding in 1870 of the Infant Life Protection Society to increasing legislative protection and greater local authority powers of intervention until the Infant Life Protection Act 1897. This was the last piece of legislation concerned solely with child protection until the Children Act 1958. Enactments in the intervening years were tacked onto omnibus legislation. (See Robert Holman, *Trading in Children: A Study of Private Fostering*, Routledge & Kegan Paul, 1973.)

8. Parker, as above.

9. Barnardo's and the Waifs and Strays Society (now The Children's Society) were something of an exception. As Parker, above, shows, a third of Barnardo's children were in foster care by 1891, although the numbers and the proportion fell back as the decade advanced.

10. Quoted, Alan A. Jacka, *The Story of the Children's Home 1869–1969*, National Children's Home, 1969. Parker, above, speculates that similar problems may have caused boarding out to start in the 1880s.

11. Parker, as above.

12. As above.

13. *Annual Report 1907–08*, NCH.

14. Parker, as above.

15. Turner and Elliott, as above.

16. As above.

17. *Annual Report 1919–20*.

18. Quoted, Jacka, as above.

19. Quoted, Bradfield.

20. Quoted, as above.

21. Quoted, Anonymous, *Sisters of the Children*, National Children's Home, 1985.

22. Quoted, *100 Years. Annual Report*, 1969.

23. Cecil Woodham Smith, *Florence Nightingale*, Constable, 1950.

24. Wagner, as above.

25. Jacka, as above.

26. Information about the Sisterhood is drawn largely from *Sisters of the Children,* as above unless otherwise stated.

27 *Year Book 1948–49*, National Children's Home.

28. For a fuller description of the later work of the Sisters, see chapter 5.

29. Bradfield, as above.

30. Quoted, Bradfield, as above.

31. Cyril Davey, *A Man for All Children: The Life of Thomas Bowman Stephenson*, Epworth Press, 1969; reprinted, NCH, 1989.

32. Quoted, Bradfield, as above.

33. As above

34. As above

5

1. The figures for children in care and income are taken from *Highways and Hedges*, November, 1900 and July, 1901, respectively. The same magazine gives the number of children as being 1,100 in 1899 (November 1899), while the July 1901 issue states that the income of £25,285 was 'less than in 1899'.

2. Official statement by the Home published as an appendix in William Bradfield, *The Life of Thomas Bowman Stephenson, BA, LLD, DD*, Charles H. Kelly, 1913.

3. *100 Years: Annual Report*, National Children's Home, 1969.

4. Cyril Davey, unpublished MS.

5. Quoted, above.

6. Quoted, above.

7. Quoted, Bradfield.

8. Quoted, Davey.

9. Alan A. Jacka, *The Story of the Children's Home 1869–1969*, National Children's Home, 1969.

10. *100 Years: Annual Report*, as above.

11. Davey, as above.

12. Phil Carradice, *A History of Headlands School 1918–1986*, unpublished MEd thesis, 1989.

13. As above.

14. Quoted, Carradice, above.

15. Julius Carlebach, *Caring for Children in Trouble*, Routledge & Kegan Paul, 1970.

16. M.A. Spielman, 'The importance of preservation of the voluntary principle in child saving and rescue work', Reformatory and Refuge Union Conference Report, 1921.

17. Quoted, Carlebach, as above.

18. Arguments about the state taking over voluntary provision did, however, become a more real argument when it came to the creation of the National Health Service in 1948. Then both local authority—the London County Council ran half the hospitals within its area—and voluntary hospitals were subsumed within a state-run structure. For a discussion of this debate see Bernard

Donoughue and G. W. Jones, *Herbert Morrison: Portrait of a Politician*, Weidenfeld & Nicolson, 1973 and Michael Foot, *Aneurin Bevan Volume 2: 1945–1960*, Davis-Poynter, 1973.

19. Ivy Pinchbeck and Margaret Hewitt, *Children in English Society, Volume 2, From the Eighteenth Century to the Children Act 1948*, Routledge & Kegan Paul, 1973.

20. Pat Turner and Jenny Elliott reported that their study of NCH adoption over a century (*Adoption—Reviewing the Record*, NCH, 1992) did not include figures prior to 1926, nor those in Scotland, and also excluded children sent to Canada, New Zealand and Australia. However, they state that over the century (1892–1982) 8,000 children have been placed, of which, they estimated, 1,000 had been placed prior to 1926 (there were 260 in 1920). (The fact that more mothers voluntarily gave up their children for adoption in the 1960s meant that between 1967 and 1969, the Home placed 1,000 children or one in eight of all those placed over the hundred years.) By comparison, in 1927 there were an estimated 1, 560 adoptions by non-relatives in England and Wales, 2,391 in 1930 and 2,567 in 1935.

21. As above.

22. Quoted, above.

23. Quoted, above.

24. Roy Parker, *Away from Home: A History of Child Care*, Barnardo's, 1990.

25. Thomas Bowman Stephenson, *The Children's Advocate*, 1873.

26. Cecil Walpole, *Any Other Business*, quoted, Anonymous, *Sisters of the Children*, National Children's Home, 1985.

27. *100 Years: Annual Report*, National Children's Home, 1969.

28. Eileen Younghusband, *Social Work in Britain: 1950–1975. A Follow Up Study, Volume 1*, Allen & Unwin, 1978.

29. Quoted, above.

30. Anonymous, *Sisters of the Children*, as above.

31. When this change occurred cannot be precisely dated but from 1944 the shorter title first appears.

32. Quoted, Davey, as above.

6

1. Quoted in Audrey O'Dell, *Burgeoning Amid the Alien Corn: New Life in a Strange Country*, privately published by the author, no date. I have drawn freely for the story of Riversmead on this book, from which quotations about the children's lives are taken.

2. The Home and Carter's Christian Council were not alone in the work of assisting refugee children. Nor were they the main source of settlement. Roy Parker (*Away from Home: A History of Child Care*, Barnardo's, 1990) states that by 1939 the Refugee Children's Movement had placed 9,000 young victims of Nazism in British foster homes.

3. William L. Shirer, *The Rise and Fall of the Third Reich*, Secker & Warburg, 1960.

4. O'Dell (above) puts the number at a million or more. When the war ended, the 28,000 Jews surviving in Germany and Austria were, largely, Jews only by the strict definition of the Nazi racial laws, according to Lucy Davidowicz, *The War Against the Jews 1933–1945*, Pelican, 1977.

5. Davidowicz, above.

7

1. R.A. Butler, *The Art of the Possible. The Memoirs of Lord Butler*, Hamish Hamilton, 1971. However, it should be added that Butler points out that when he drafted the Bill, no other minister on the home front had been able to bring his plans to fruition.

2. A.J.P. Taylor, *English History 1914–1945*, Oxford University Press, 1965.

3. Alan A. Jacka, *The Story of the Children's Home 1869–1969*, National Children's Home, 1969.

4. John H.Litten, *Blueprints. The Reconstruction Plans of the National Children's Home*, National Children's Home, 1943.

5. As above.

6. *Year Book 1947–48*, NCH.

7. As above.

8. *The Times*, 15 July 1944.

9. Lady Allen of Hurtwood, *Whose Children?*, 1945.

10. June Rose, *For the Sake of the Children. Inside Barnardo's: 120 Years of Caring for Children*, Hodder & Stoughton, 1987.

11. Curtis Committee, *Report of the Care of Children Committee*, HMSO, 1946.

12. Thomas Bowman Stephenson, *The Children's Advocate*, 1873.

13. Curtis Committee, as above.

14. Barnardo's report on the Care of Children Committee, 1946, quoted by Rose, above.

15. *Year Book 1947–48*, as above.

16. Eileen Younghusband, *Social Work in Britain: 1950- -1975. A Follow Up Study* Volume 1, George Allen & Unwin, 1979.

17. *Year Book 1947–48*, as above.

18. Younghusband, as above.

19. Pat Taylor and Jenny Elliott, *Adoption— Reviewing the Record*, NCH, 1992.

20. *100 Years: Annual Report*, Natiomal Children's Home, 1969.

21. *Annual Report*, National Children's Home, 1967 and *Year Book*, National Children's Home, 1968.

22. *106. Annual Report*, National Children's Home, 1975.

23. *107. Annual Report*, National Children's Home, 1976.

24. *100 Years: Annual Report*, as above.

25. *Annual Report,* 1967 and *Year Book* 1968, as above.

26. *106. Annual Report*, as above.

27. David Benger, quoted by Phil Carradice, *A History of Headlands School 1918–1986*, unpublished MEd thesis, 1969.

28. Younghusband, as above.

29. Longford committee, *Crime: A Challenge to Us All*, Labour Party, 1964.

30. Home Office, *The Child, The Family and the Young Offender*, HMSO, 1965.

31. Home Office, *Children in Trouble*, HMSO, 1968.

32. As above.

33. Phil Carradice, as above.

34. Social Care Association, *The Bonnington Report*, Social Care Association, 1984.

35. Cyril Davey, unpublished MS.

36. As above.

37. Jacka, as above.

8

1. Virginia Membrey, 'Care in the sun', *Community Care*, 21 July 1988.

2. *Year Book*, 1971.

3. 'Plight of teenage girls in Belize', *NCH News*, March, 1993.

4. 'NCH in Zimbabwe', *NCH News*, November/December 1990.

5. Membrey, as above.

6. Communication from Tom White to author, 22 March 1994.

7. Internal paper on overseas work by the principal to social work committee of NCH, 20 November 1990.

8. As above.

9 Calderdale

1. Fran Orford, 'Leaving care', unpublished paper, undated.

2. *First Key*, survey of local authority provision for young people leaving care, commissioned by the Department of Health, 1993.

9 Glasgow

1. *The Chinese Community in Britain*, three volumes, HMSO, 1985.

9 Manchester

1. Janet Walker, Peter McCarthy and Judy Corlyon, *Mediation: The Making and*

Remaking of Co-Operative Relationships—An Evaluation of the Effectiveness of Comprehensive Mediation, University of Newcastle, 1994.

2. Quoted in *Children Come First. The Case for Conciliation,* NCH, 1991.

3. As above.

4. National Family Conciliation Council, *Research on Children's Experience of Divorce.* Factsheet. Undated.

9 South Glamorgan

1. *Confined to the Community,* 1991, available free from Options, 56 Conybeare Road, Canton, Cardiff DF5 1GF. See also section on Llanrumney Community Project above.

9 Strathclyde

1. H. Kempe, F.N. Silverway, B.F. Steele, W. Dreoegemueller, and H.K. Silver, 'The battered child syndrome', *Journal of the American Medical Association,* 181 (i), 1962.

2. *Report of the Committee of Inquiry into the Care and Supervision Provided in Relation to Maria Colwell,* HMSO, 1974.

3. *Survey of Treatment Facilities for Abused Children and Facilities for Young Abusers of Children,* NCH, 1990.

4. Royal Scottish Society for the Prevention of Cruelty to Children, Overnewton Centre, *Working with Families where Child Abuse has Occurred. A Memo of Practice 1987–1991,* undated. This work has now been absorbed by Strathclyde social work department.

5. E.Butler-Sloss, *The Report of the Inquiry into Child Abuse in Cleveland 1987,* HMSO, 1988.

6. I am grateful to Greg Gallagher, principal officer, Strathclyde Regional Social Work Department for the figures regarding his region.

7. Barbara Kelly and Malcolm Hill, *Children and Families Counselling Project Report,* NCH Action For Children, 1994.

8. See, V. Prior, M. Lynch, D. Glaser, *Messages From Children: Children's Evaluations of the*

Professional Response to Child Sexual Abuse: Interim Report, NCH Action For Children, July 1994.

9 Suffolk

1. Home Office, *Prison Statistics. England and Wales 1992,* HMSO, 1994.

2. Klapmusts, quoted, P. Jones, 'Expanding the use of non-custodial sentencing options: An evaluation of the Kansas Community Correction Act', *Howard Journal,* Vol 29, No 2, 1990.

3. Ian Brownlee and Derrick Joannes, *Leeds Young Adult Offenders Projects. A Second Evaluation Report 1990–1991,* Faculty of Law, University of Leeds, 1991. This project closed in March 1994 with the withdrawal of the Home Office's grant.

9 Sutton Coldfield

1. NCH Action For Children regional office, a study centre and a family placement unit also stands on the site.

2. The high number of hours worked is connected with NCH Action For Children's concern about how local authorities have emulated industrial practices in residential care (but usually without paying salaries commensurate with the stress and responsibilities of residential work, whatever the hours). The reason for the 45-hour week is to provide greater continuity of care for the children, to ensure that on most occasions the same person is in the home both at the time that the child goes to bed and when he or she is woken in the morning.

10

1. Terry Philpot, 'An emerging principal' (profile), *Community Care,* 26 July, 1984.

2. Barbara Castle, *The Castle Diaries 1974–1976,* Weidenfeld & Nicolson, 1980. See also, Terry Philpot, 'Tom, Tom the miner's son'

(profile), *Community Care*, 23 May, 1985.

3. Roger Bullock, *Residential Care for Children*, NCH, 1992.

4. For a concise summary, see Bullock, above.

5. Jane Rowe and Lydia Lambert, *Children Who Wait*, Association of British Adoption Agencies, 1973.

6. For a description of the state of residential care generally over the past decade, see Terry Philpot, 'Overview', *Positive Answers: Final Report of the Wagner Development Group*, HMSO, 1993.

7. Tom White, 'Dear Adrianne...', *Community Care*, 10 June, 1993.

8. NCH, *Left to Their Own Devices, A Report on Youth Homelessness*, NCH, 1990.

9. *Young People and Severe Hardship*, Coalition on Young People and Social Security, 1990.

10. NCH, *Housing Vulnerable, Young, Single, Homeless People*, NCH, 1987.

11. Quotations taken from *Left to Their Own Devices*, NCH, 1990, above.

12. NCH, London Housing Unit and SHAC, *Your Place or Mine?*, NCH, 1993.

13. Jean Moore, *The ABC of Child Child Abuse Work*, Gower/*Community Care*, 1985. See also the same author's *The ABC of Child Protection*, Ashgate, 1992.

14. NCH,*Children Sexually Abusing Other Children—The Last Taboo?*, NCH, 1991.

15. Quoted, NCH press release, 24 April, 1992.

16. Quoted, NCH, *Child Sexual Abuse. 10 Facts*, NCH, undated. Actual incidence of all forms of abuse (much of it unknown and unregistered) can only be guessed. The NSPCC estimates, using its own registers, that the number of children physically injured in 1990 in England and Wales as 10,100 (a fall of 400 on the previous year), with a total of 34,700 registrations (a fall of 1,600 on the previous year). (See Susan J. Creighton, *Child Abuse Trends in England and Wales 1988–1990*, NSPCC, 1992.)

17. *The Times*, 3 March, 1993.

18. Letter, *The Guardian*, 3 March, 1993.

19. 'Charities spurn "borstal" plan', news story, *The Guardian*, 1 April 1993.

20. 'Setting the record straight: Juvenile crime in perspective.' A memorandum by NCH to the House of Commons Home Affairs Select Committee, January, 1993.

21. Quoted, above.

22. Mark Ivory, 'Cry freedom', *Community Care*, 10 June 1993.

23. While keeping families together is the theory and often the practice of social work, it is also the case that the large rise in the use of place of safety orders and increased numbers of children on child abuse registers followed the need to play safe. The number of place of safety orders taken out trebled during the 1970s following the Colwell inquiry of 1974 and increased again from a rate of 0.45 per 1,000 (0–17) to 0.73 in 1987 and 0.71 in 1988. The number of children on NSPCC registers more than doubled between 1983 and 1987, with a twelve-fold increase in registered cases of sexual abuse. (Figures from various sources quoted by Bob Franklin and Nigel Parton, 'Media reporting of social work: A framework for analysis', in Bob Franklin and Nigel Parton (editors), *Social Work, The Media and Public Relations*, Routledge, 1991.)

24. Roy Parker (editor), *Caring for Separated Children: Plans, Procedures and Priorities*, Macmillan, 1980.

25. See Bob Holman, *Putting Families First. Prevention and Child Care: A Study of Prevention by Statutory and Voluntary Agencies*, Macmillan, 1988.

26. Quoted, Crecy Cannan, *Changing Families, Changing Welfare. Family Centres and the Welfare State*, Harvester-Wheatsheaf, 1992.

27. As above.

28. H.Frayman, *Breadline Britain in the 1990s: The Findings of the Television Series*, Domino Films/London Weekend Television, 1991. According to the House of Commons Library (1993) 2,970,000 children live in families receiving Income Support, or nearly one in four children in Britain. In 1990–1991 3.3 million dependent children were living in

households in the bottom 20 per cent of income distribution in Britain (*Households Below Average Income*, Department of Social Security, 1993).

29. *Social Trends*, HMSO, 1994.

30. Quoted, *The NCH Fact File*, 1993.

31. Quoted, Cannan, above.

32. NCH, 'NCH family centre policy', report to the social work committee, March, 1992.

33. NCH, 'The place of community work in NCH', report to the social work committee, 8 May 1990.

34. NCH, *Poverty and Nutrition Survey*, 1991.

35. As above.

36. Office of Population, Censuses and Surveys, *Survey of Disability*, HMSO, 1989.

37. NCH Action For Children, *Unequal Opportunities—Children with Disabilities andTheir Families Speak Out*, NCH Action For Children, 1994.

38. Quoted, as above.

11

1. Roy Parker, *Away from Home: A History of Child Care,* Barnardo's, 1990.

2. National Children's Home, *Annual Report 1899–1900.*

3. NCH, 'NCH's Foundation, purpose and values', 10 February 1992.

4. H. Frayman, *Breadline Britain in the 1990s: The Findings of the Television Series,* Domino Films/London Weekend Television, 1991.

5. Shelter, 1993, quoted, *NCH Fact File*, 1993.

6. Young Homeless Group, Centrepoint, 1992, quoted, *NCH Fact File*, 1993.

7. CHAR, quoted, *NCH Fact File*, 1993.

8. Parker, as above.

Index

Also from Lion Publishing:

A New Deal for Social Welfare

Bob Holman

Are we creating a cash-register society?

Social workers have become case managers.

Local authorities increasingly buy and sell welfare services.

It's the contract culture: social services in the marketplace.

Bob Holman, former Professor of Social Administration at the University of Bath, has been a welfare worker for over 20 years. He regularly contributes to professional journals, *The Guardian* and other magazines. And he lives on a large, mainly council, housing scheme in Glasgow amongst many people who depend on welfare services.

This book is a powerful analysis of the theories which are transforming social welfare from being a 'caring profession' to a buying-and-selling business. It is also a passionate plea for welfare to adopt new principles and practices.

ISBN 0 7459 2848 X